Financial Accounting

A Course for All Majors

Financial Accounting

A Course for All Majors

by

David W. O'Bryan
Pittsburg State University

Information Age Publishing, Inc.
Charlotte, North Carolina • www.infoagepub.com

Library of Congress Cataloging-in-Publication Data

O'Bryan, David W.
Financial accounting : a course for all majors / by David W. O'Bryan.
p. cm.
Includes bibliographical references.
ISBN 978-1-61735-095-5 (pbk.) -- ISBN 978-1-61735-096-2 (hardcover) --
ISBN 978-1-61735-097-9 (e-book)
1. Accounting. I. Title.
HF5636.O27 2010
657--dc22

2010021953

Printed in the United States of America

Dedication

This book is dedicated to my daughters, Jenny and Sarah. If you think you have a better way of doing something, find a way to try it. If you fail, keep trying. Nothing ventured, nothing gained. Please don't accept the status quo when you know you could do better.

CONTENTS

FOREWORD

The idea for this book arose out of frustration with current products on the market. Although the financial accounting market segment is crowded, none of the existing books are a good fit for a general education course with students from all majors.

Most of the financial accounting textbooks on the market are designed for the *first course in financial accounting for an accounting major.* The primary purpose of this first course is to prepare accounting majors for subsequent courses in their major. The fact that the majority of students in the class are nonaccounting business majors or nonbusiness majors is not a concern; the perspective seems to be that it won't "hurt" these students to be exposed to some additional technical detail. If this philosophy fits your vision for your course, this book is not for you.

This book is designed for the *only course in financial accounting that the students may ever take.* With this perspective, we would like the course to be accessible to students from all majors so that they will comprehend the material, complete the course, and enhance their financial literacy. If improving the financial literacy of all students in your class is a goal for your course, then our textbook is the right choice for you.

A skeptic might conclude that our product is simply diluted so that students can complete the course but not really know anything about financial accounting. This depends upon what you mean by "knowing" something about financial accounting. If this means the student could complete the accounting cycle for a small business then our course is probably not for you. If, instead, "knowing" means the student understands the basic premises underlying the accrual basis of accounting and the three major financial statements then we believe our course will produce students who know plenty about financial accounting.

This textbook was not designed to be the first course in financial accounting for accounting majors. However, if accounting majors learn all the material in this book then they will have the necessary conceptual foundation to succeed in their major. We have used this material in two completely online courses and in four traditional class offerings beginning in 2006. We have now had time to follow the accounting majors through their accounting courses and can report that all of them have stated they were at least as well prepared, if not more so, than their colleagues who had a more traditional financial accounting course.

This textbook was designed to be a focused, streamlined product. It contains 24 chapters, but each chapter is relatively brief. The intent was to deliver a product that was crisp and concise so that students would actually read the material. The writing style is intentionally informal and anecdotal in nature to convince students that financial accounting is accessible to them if only they will make a reasonable effort to read and study the material.

Finally, we want to state at the outset that this textbook does not utilize debit and credits. We do include an appendix on debits and credits that is intended to serve as a bridge for those students who will be taking subsequent accounting courses. There are ample arguments for using, or not using, debits and credits in the first accounting course. Our book is simply for those who believe a course in financial accounting can be effective without debit and credits.

OVERVIEW OF TEXTBOOK

MODULE I: CHAPTERS 1–5

Chapter 1 provides an overview of the accounting profession so that students will have a view of the "big picture." We want them to realize that although Financial Accounting is the foundation for much of what we do in accounting, it is not all that we do in accounting.

Chapter 2 introduces the three basic financial statements, namely the Balance Sheet, Income Statement, and Statement of Cash Flows.

Chapter 3 utilizes the concept of the expanded accounting equation to distinguish among the components of equity. We also utilize subcategories of the cash account to illustrate how operating, investing, and financing cash flows are classified on the Statement of Cash Flows. Our philosophy and rationale for using this approach is explained in more detail in O'Bryan, Berry, Troutman, and Quirin (2000).

Chapter 4 introduces transaction analysis using the expanded accounting equation. Importantly, we do so in the context of all cash transactions. We defer the discussion of the accrual basis of accounting, accruals and deferrals until Chapter 6.

Chapter 5 shows how the three financial statements are interrelated. By the conclusion of Chapter 5 we would expect students to know the components of the three major financial statements and how basic cash transactions affect the three financial statements.

MODULE II: CHAPTER 6–12

Chapter 6 introduces the accrual basis of accounting and the related credit transactions. Chapter 7 discusses the terminology of accruals and deferrals.

Chapters 8 and 9 explain adjusting entries. This is typically one of the more difficult topics for students so we divide this material into two chapters and use several approaches to help them understand this material.

Chapter 10 provides an overview of the accounting cycle. Our approach here is intentionally conceptual and is not designed for preparers.

Chapter 11 covers the classified balance sheet and Chapter 12 concludes Module II with an overview of the multiple-step income statement.

By the conclusion of Module II we would expect students to understand the basic premises underlying the accrual basis of accounting, including the adjustment process, and know the steps in the accounting cycle. They should also know the common categories on a classified balance sheet and the format of a multiple-step income statement.

MODULE III: CHAPTER 13–18

Chapters 13-17 focus on operating-type activities and Chapter 18 on investing-type activities. Chapters 13 and 14 primarily focus on accounting for bad debts. We discuss the direct write-off method as a means to frame the need for the allowance method. Within the allowance method we cover the basic approach to estimating bad debts using both the income statement and balance sheet approaches. However, we only cover cases where the Allowance for Bad Debts has an existing normal, credit balance. This is our compromise between not covering the Allowance method at all in this course versus more complete coverage including the cases where the Allowance account has an existing debit balance.

Chapter 15 discusses of revenue recognition. Since so many difficult issues in Financial Accounting revolve around revenue recognition, we feel that a basic course for all majors should highlight the common schemes employed to inappropriately recognize revenue.

Chapters 16 and 17 focus primarily on inventory cost flow assumptions. We cover FIFO, LIFO and average cost in the context of a periodic inventory system. Although perpetual inventory systems are the norm, we utilize the periodic system so that we can concentrate on the basic differences among the cost flow assumptions and not get distracted by the bookkeeping details inherent in doing perpetual inventory calculations manually in the classroom.

Chapter 18 is the sole chapter on investing-type activities and primarily discusses allocating costs of long-term assets. To maintain focus and our conceptual approach, we only cover straight-line depreciation/amortization in this chapter.

After completing Module III students should know the most common accounting issues in the operating cycle (i.e., bad debts and inventory costing), appreciate the complexities associated with revenue recognition, and have a solid understanding of allocating the costs of long-term assets.

MODULE IV: CHAPTERS 19–24

Chapters 19-21 cover financing-type activities. Chapter 19 begins with simple interest and amortized loans. Corporate bond terminology and pricing are covered in a separate section of Chapter 19 for those who prefer to omit this topic from the course.

Chapter 20 covers the time value of money using the financial functions in Excel to solve common time value of money problems. Determining the price of a corporate bond using Excel is covered in a separate section for those who do not wish to cover bonds in this course.

Chapter 21 covers equity transactions including dividends, stock splits and treasury stock.

Chapters 22 and 23 provide an introduction to financial statement analysis. We do not attempt to cover all ratios here but do cover at least one in each major category. And, we try to frame the discussion of ratio analysis in this class as a subset of ratios (e.g., miles per gallon, grade point average) commonly encountered in daily life.

Chapter 24 concludes this Module with a discussion of internal controls. We believe it is critical for students to understand the motivation for internal controls and the accountant's role in helping an organization safeguard assets with an effective system of internal controls.

Chapters 19-21 should leave students with a solid grasp of the key issues involved in accounting for financing type activities, including practical applications of the time value of money. The coverage of financial statement analysis in Chapters 22 and 23 is intended to provide students some sense of how the information in financial statements can be used for decision making. Finally, we hope students appreciate the importance of internal controls after reading Chapter 24.

Appendix I: Debits and Credits: Appendix I provides basic coverage of the terminology of debit and credits, the proper formatting of journal entries, and the use of T-accounts. This Appendix is intended to be a bridge, or transition, for those students who will be taking subsequent accounting courses.

Appendix II: Transaction Analysis Quick Reference Guide: Since transaction analysis is often one of the more difficult components of this course, we provide Appendix II to supplement our coverage of this topic and to provide students with a quick reference guide for reviewing transaction analysis.

TEXTBOOK SUPPLEMENT

A set of approximately 20 objective questions to accompany each chapter are available in electronic format to those who adopt this textbook. These questions may be downloaded at: http://www.insertwebsitehere.com.

REFERENCE

O'Bryan, D., K. Berry, C. Troutman, & J. Quirin. (2000). Using accounting equation analysis to teach the statement of cash flows in the first financial accounting course. *Journal of Accounting Education, 18,* 147-155.

ACKNOWLEDGMENTS

This book would not have been possible without the supportive environment at Pittsburg State University where the author was given the autonomy to experiment with a new approach to the first course in financial accounting. The contents have benefitted greatly from student feedback the past few years. The positive feedback from former students has been especially helpful in motivating me to publish this material. Information Age Publishing is providing me with an opportunity to share this work with others and, importantly to this author, do so at an affordable price for students. Finally, I want to thank my family for giving me the time to complete this project.

CHAPTER 1

THE ACCOUNTING PROFESSION

An Overview

INTRODUCTION

Most Financial Accounting books are written primarily for accounting or business majors. This book is written for all majors. We hope our approach helps more people learn financial accounting, especially those who might otherwise struggle or give up in a traditional offering of Financial Accounting.

AN OVERVIEW OF THE ACCOUNTING PROFESSION

The title of this course is Financial Accounting. To put this in context, we are going to begin by talking about the accounting profession in general. Financial accounting is arguably the foundation for all of accounting, but it is nevertheless just a subset of the broader field of accounting. The outline that follows will provide you with an overall view of the accounting profession.

Financial Accounting: A Course for All Majors, pp. 1–4

1. Financial Accounting—the title of this course. This area of accounting includes the fundamental bookkeeping of an organization, but is much broader in the sense that it culminates in the publication of a set of reports, called financial statements, that summarize the financial results for an entity for a particular period of time.

   (a) The financial statements are primarily produced for *external* parties who otherwise would not be able to obtain financial information about the entity. For example, if you own stock in a company like Wal-Mart your primary source of information about the company's financial performance is from their financial statements.
   (b) An entity could be an individual, a company, a church, or any organization that depends upon economic resources.

2. Managerial Accounting—is typically required for all business majors and is taken after Financial Accounting. Managerial accounting focuses upon the informational needs of those working within the company. A common distinction between Financial and Managerial Accounting is that Financial Accounting is primarily directed toward external parties, while Managerial Accounting is primarily directed toward internal parties.
3. Auditing—conjures up images of being investigated by the Internal Revenue Service. Sure enough, this is one example of auditing. However, auditing is broader in the sense that it involves reviewing and critiquing what others have done. In this sense, auditing could be compared to a teacher grading homework. There are two, major subsets of auditing.

   (a) Internal Auditors—work for a single entity and spend their time reviewing the processes and operations of that entity on a full-time basis. For example, a large company like Verizon has a dedicated staff of internal auditors who work for the company on a full-time basis.
   (b) External Auditors—work for a public accounting firm and serve multiple clients. External auditors typically are hired to review a company's financial statements and express an overall judgment, or opinion, as to whether the financial statements fairly present the entity's financial results and position. For example, a large company like Sprint has internal auditors that work for it full-time throughout the year, but at least annually they will also hire an external

auditor to review their financial statements. The external auditor adds value by providing an independent review of the work done throughout the year by the company's own employees. The overall goal is to help make sure the financial statements, the output of the Financial Accounting process, are accurate and complete.

(i) What is a public accounting firm? A public accounting firm is a separate entity that provides accounting, tax, auditing, and other related services to customers. Just as your dentist provides dental services to many different patients, a public accounting provides its services to many different clients and not just one company.

4. Taxation—this is the subset of accounting that most people are familiar with because most of us have to file an income tax return and pay income taxes. **This course is not directed toward helping you prepare your income tax return!** As odd as it may sound, the rules used in Financial Accounting are *not* always the same rules that we are required to use when filing our income tax return.
5. Accounting Information Systems—this subset of accounting deals with the design and implementation of the systems used to accumulate all the various economic transactions that affect an entity. The accounting profession is heavily reliant on computers and technology to make our work more efficient and effective. A person who specializes in accounting information systems is typically well versed in both accounting and computer information systems.
6. Emerging Careers—although many reading this textbook may not be accounting majors, some will nevertheless still be searching for a promising degree choice. With this in mind, we will mention some areas within the accounting profession that are in high demand.

(a) Internal auditing—because of corporate scandals like WorldCom and Enron, some newer federal regulations have created a shortage of internal auditors. Internal auditors are typically exposed to many different facets of an organization so it can be an excellent place for a new employee to begin their career.
(b) Forensic accountants—these people specialize in using accounting information as evidence in legal proceedings. Often times, they are investigating fraudulent activities and financial crimes. Other times they are simply following a

money trail to make sure that their client is treated fairly. For example, a good friend of mine works divorce cases and helps make sure that his client gets his or her fair share of the marital assets.

(c) Information Technology, or IT, Auditors—typically these people are double majors in accounting and information systems. In an increasingly computer-driven world, these people audit computer systems. For example, the online brokerage company TD Ameritrade is heavily dependent on its online trading system to serve its customers. It has a relatively large staff of IT Auditors who strive to maintain the efficiency and effectiveness of that online trading system. They also have to make sure the system is safe and secure.

SUMMARY

The accounting profession includes Financial Accounting, Managerial Accounting, Auditing, Taxation, and Accounting Information Systems. This is summarized in Figure 1.1.

The title of our course is Financial Accounting so Chapter 2 will sharpen the focus on this subset of the accounting profession. Please keep in mind that although the remainder of this course will focus mostly on Financial Accounting, this is just one subset of the broader area known as "accounting."

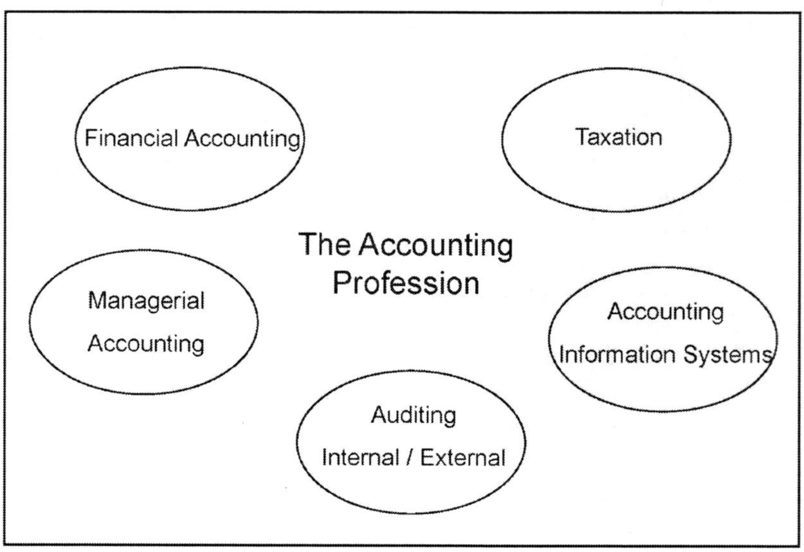

Figure 1.1. An Overview of the Accounting Profession.

CHAPTER 2

THREE BASIC FINANCIAL STATEMENTS

INTRODUCTION

In Chapter 1 we learned that Financial Accounting is a subset of the broader field of accounting. This chapter will now sharpen our focus on the primary focus of this course, Financial Accounting.

FINANCIAL ACCOUNTING

We are going to start with a very basic definition of Financial Accounting as a "black box" that converts inputs into outputs:

Inputs → Financial Accounting → Outputs

In this diagram, the basic inputs are the multitude of economic transactions that affect an entity. For example, think of the, literally, millions of cash register transactions for Wal-Mart in any given year. These are the basic inputs into the Financial Accounting process.

The outputs of the Financial Accounting process are a set of reports that summarize the financial results and position of an entity for a particular time period. These reports are called *financial statements.*

Financial Accounting: A Course for All Majors, pp. 5–13

How do we get from inputs to outputs? What is in the black box? Well, for this class we won't worry too much about understanding the technical details that take place in the black box. Accounting majors will study that in great detail in a future class. For now, we will focus on understanding how the inputs (i.e., financial transactions) affect the outputs (i.e., financial statements).

FINANCIAL STATEMENTS

If you think about condensing the information from potentially millions of transactions (the inputs) into a few reports (the outputs) you will quickly realize that financial statements are a summary of economic activity for a period of time. In fact, this is one of the primary benefits of financial statements. If you are thinking about buying stock in Wal-Mart, or if a bank were thinking about lending them money, you probably don't need to review every single cash register transaction. You do need to know whether they are making money from their day-to-day operations, whether they can repay their debts, or whether they can pay their day-to-day costs as they come due.

There are three, primary financial statements. The remainder of this chapter will introduce these financial statements and the related concepts that accompany each statement.

THE BALANCE SHEET

The very name of this statement implies that something "balances", that something equals something else. Let's cut to the chase and look at the fundamental equation underlying the balance sheet:

The Accounting Equation: Assets = Liabilities + Equity

This equation underlies much of what we will do in Financial Accounting. You should memorize it now. Please note that this is merely an algebra equation stating that the term on the left, Assets, must always equal the summation of the terms on the right, Liabilities and Equity. Like any algebra equation this can also be rewritten as follows:

The Accounting Equation – Alternative Forms: Assets – Liabilities = Equity or Assets – Equity = Liabilities

Now, let's examine each element of the balance sheet in more detail.

Assets

Most people have an intuitive understanding of this term. Assets are things with future, economic benefits. That's a fancy way of saying they are things with value. Examples of assets include cash, vehicles, houses, land, and the computer I'm using to prepare this chapter.

Liabilities

Most people have an even better understanding of this term! Liabilities are amounts we owe, or debts. Examples of liabilities include student loans, credit card debt, and car loans.

Equity

Of the three terms, assets, liabilities, and equity, this is the least intuitive of the three. Let's repeat an earlier version of The Accounting Equation:

Assets – Liabilities = Equity

In this equation, Equity is what's left over after subtracting Liabilities from Assets. For example, if you own a car that is worth \$15,000, and you owe \$9,000 on it, what is your equity in the car?

$$\$15,000 - \$9,000 = ?$$

Your equity in the car is \$6,000. So, one way to define Equity is that it is what remains after subtracting Liabilities from Assets. Equity represents your ownership interest in an Asset or collection of Assets.

There are several synonyms for Equity. First, if we are talking about the Equity of an individual or household we often use the term Net Worth. Second, if we are talking about the Equity of a company we might use the term Stockholders' Equity, because the owners of a company are called stockholders.

The Balance Sheet summarizes what you have (Assets), what you owe (Liabilities) and what you're worth (Equity) at any given point in time. It is a snapshot of your financial position at a specific date and time.

THE INCOME STATEMENT

The second financial statement is The Income Statement. The algebra equation underlying this statement is:

Revenues – Expenses = Net Income

Revenues

Revenues are things we receive in exchange for providing goods or services to others. For an individual, the primary way we earn Revenue is by providing our services (i.e., labor) to others in exchange for a paycheck. For a business, Revenue is earned by providing a good or service in exchange for payment now, or the promise of payment in the future.

Expenses

Expenses are the costs we incur to help us earn Revenues. For an individual, these include all the day-to-day costs we are so familiar with—food, clothing, shelter, gasoline, and so forth. For a business, these include all the costs of providing a good or service for customers.

Net Income

As you can see in the equation above, Net Income is what remains after subtracting Expenses from Revenues. Net Income is the primary measure used in Financial Accounting to determine whether we are making money.

There are several synonyms for Net Income. These include Earnings, Profits, and "the bottom line". The latter term comes from the fact that an income statement is normally displayed in vertical format, with the Revenues first, followed by the Expenses, and last, the Net Income at the bottom. If it is your personal or business Income Statement, you certainly hope that there is something leftover on "the bottom line" after subtracting Expenses from Revenues!

THE STATEMENT OF CASH FLOWS

The third financial statement is The Statement of Cash Flows. In its most basic form, this statement summarizes the cash going into and out of your bank account.

Beginning Cash + Increase (– Decrease) in Cash = Ending Cash where Increase (Decrease) in Cash = Change in Cash

Let's consider an example where our beginning cash balance is $100, our cash balance increased by $150 during the year, and our ending cash balance is therefore $250. A visual representation follows in Figure 2.1

So, The Statement of Cash Flows is pretty intuitive because it deals with something we are all quite familiar with—money flowing into and out of a bank account. Now, what most students are completely unfamiliar with are the categories used to discuss cash inflows and cash outflows on The Statement of Cash Flows.

Before we introduce these new terms, let's think about the typical steps involved in starting a new business. Let's assume a person has an idea for a product or service that they would like to sell to others.

Step 1 is to figure out where to get some money so that we can produce the product, or provide the service. Let's refer to this as the *Financing*

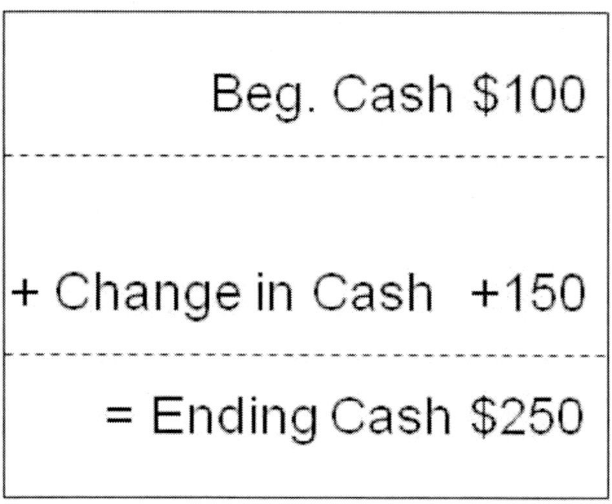

Figure 2.1. A Very Basic View of the Statement of Cash Flows.

decision. There are basically two ways to finance the business—debt or equity. That is, we can either borrow money (debt) or we can use our own money (equity).

Step 2 is to use these funds to buy the assets we need to be able to provide a good or service to our customers. It depends on the business, but we might need to buy buildings, land, equipment, vehicles or a host of other items so that we can begin selling to our customers. This is referred to as the *Investing* decision.

Step 3 is to commence the day-to-day operations of the new business. This is the *Operating* decision, or phase of the process. To recap, first we raised some money to get started in the Financing phase. Then, we used that money to buy the assets we needed in the Investment phase. Finally, we were ready to start providing a good or service to our customer in the Operating phase.

The Statement of Cash Flows organizes the cash inflows and cash outflows into these three categories: Operating, Investing, and Financing. We will briefly discuss the typical items represented in each category.

Financing Cash Flows

Financing cash inflows are monies received from borrowing (i.e., debt) or money received from the owners (i.e., equity). Financing cash outflows are monies used by the business to repay debt or to return some money to the owners.

Note here that we are treating the business as an entity separate and distinct from its owners. This is called the *Entity Concept*. Even if the business only has one owner, you, we still view the business separately from your personal activities and we recommend you keep the business activities separate from your personal activities.

Investing Cash Flows

Investing cash outflows are monies used to acquire other assets. Let's pause here. An Asset is something with future economic value. Is a paper clip an Asset? Technically, it probably is, but it is a relatively insignificant item with a relatively short life. What we are primarily talking about with Investing activities are significant assets with a relatively long life, defined as more than one year. This would include buying things like land, buildings, equipment, machinery, vehicles, furniture, or computers. Investing cash inflows would be monies received from later selling these assets.

Operating Cash Flows

Operating cash inflows are the monies received from customers as a result of providing them with goods or services. Operating cash outflows are the monies used to pay for the many costs we will incur to be able to provide goods or services to our customers.

Now, let's revisit the example from Figure 2.1. Let's think about the $150 increase in cash first. Think about your checking account and recognize that your account goes up because of deposits, or cash inflows, and goes down when you spend money, or cash outflows. Let's assume that for this example the total cash inflows were $650 and the total cash outflows were –$500, with the net result being that our cash account increased by $150 during the year. This is illustrated in Figure 2.2.

Now, let's decompose the $650 total cash inflows into the three categories Operating, Investing, and Financing. For our example we will assume the company had a $600 cash inflow from Operating activities, $0 from Investing activities, and $50 from Financing activities. We can also categorize the – $500 total cash outflows into the same three categories. For this example, we will assume the company had a – $400 cash outflow from Operating activities, – $100 from Investing activities, and $0 from Financing activities.

Figure 2.3 illustrates this new way of looking at the $150 increase in cash. It shows that the total cash inflows are still $650 but we now report them in three categories; likewise, the total cash outflows are still -$500, but they are also reported in three categories.

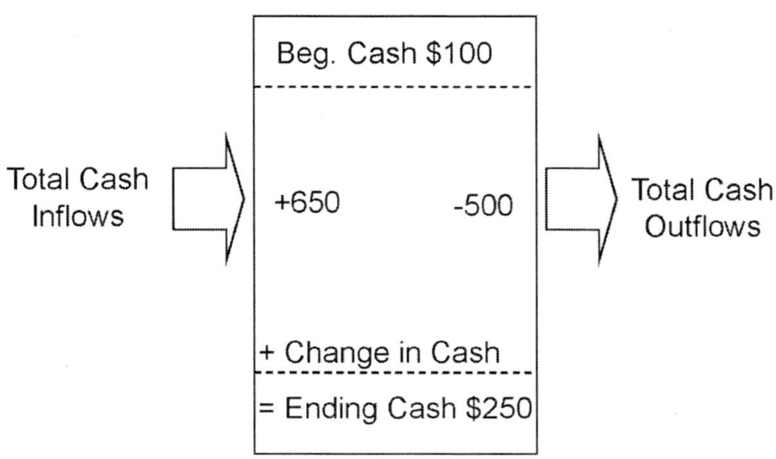

Figure 2.2. The Concept of "Flows" in the Statement of Cash Flows.

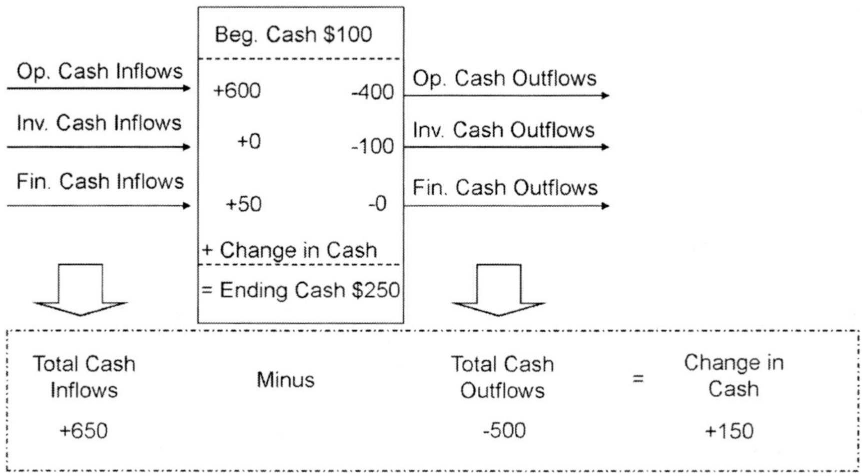

Figure 2.3. Categories of Cash Flows in the Statement of Cash Flows.

Now, let's add the concept of "Net" cash flows:

Operating Cash Inflows - Operating Cash Outflows = Net Operating Cash Flows Investing Cash Inflows - Investing Cash Outflows = Net Investing Cash Flows Financing Cash Inflows – Financing Cash Outflows = Net Financing Cash Flows

We have one final point to make about the Statement of Cash Flows and we will conclude this chapter.

Net Operating Cash Flows + Net Investing Cash Flows + Net Financing Cash Flows = Increase (Decrease) in Cash

These concepts are illustrated in Figure 2.4. Looking at the illustration horizontally we can see the net cash flows for Operating, Investing, and Financing activities. If we look at the right-hand side of figure from a vertical perspective we can see that summing the three net cash flows equals the $150 increase in cash for the period.

The Statement of Cash Flows explains the change in cash by using the terminology of cash inflows and cash outflows and then further classifies the cash inflows and cash outflows into three categories: Operating,

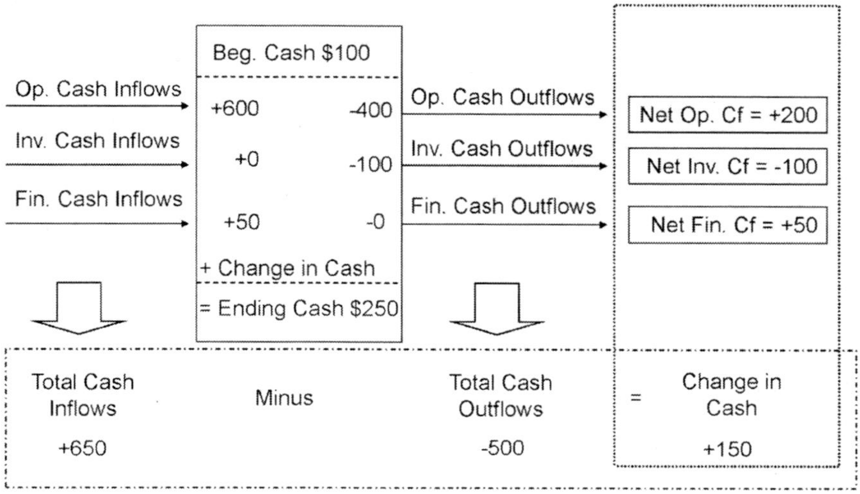

Figure 2.4. A Graphical Representation of the Statement of Cash Flows.

Investing, or Financing. By doing so the Statement of Cash Flows explains why the cash account changed during the period.

SUMMARY

This chapter has introduced the three, major financial statements used in Financial Accounting and the related algebra equation(s) underlying each statement, which we summarize below:

1. The Balance Sheet: Assets = Liabilities + Equity
2. The Income Statement: Revenues-Expenses = Net Income
3. The Statement of Cash Flows:

3A. Operating Cash Inflows – Operating Cash Outflows = Net Operating Cash Flows
3B. Investing Cash Inflows – Investing Cash Outflows = Net Investing Cash Flows
3C. Financing Cash Inflows – Financing Cash Outflows = Net Financing Cash Flows
3D. Net Operating Cash Flows + Net Investing Cash Flows + Net Financing Cash Flows = Increase (Decrease) in Cash
3E. Beginning Cash + Increase (– Decrease) in Cash = Ending Cash

CHAPTER 3

THE EXPANDED ACCOUNTING EQUATION

INTRODUCTION

In Chapter 1 we learned that Financial Accounting is a subset of the broader field of accounting. Chapter 2 discussed the three, major financial statements: The Balance Sheet, The Income Statement, and The Statement of Cash Flows. There are several important algebra equations from Chapter 2 which we repeat for your convenience below.

1. The Balance Sheet: Assets = Liabilities + Equity
2. The Income Statement: Revenues – Expenses = Net Income
3. The Statement of Cash Flows:

3A. Operating Cash Inflows – Operating Cash Outflows = Net Operating Cash Flows
3B. Investing Cash Inflows – Investing Cash Outflows = Net Investing Cash Flows
3C. Financing Cash Inflows – Financing Cash Outflows = Net Financing Cash Flows
3D. Net Operating Cash Flows + Net Investing Cash Flows + Net Financing Cash Flows = Increase (Decrease) in Cash
3E. Beginning Cash + Increase (– Decrease) in Cash = Ending Cash

Financial Accounting: A Course for All Majors, pp. 15–23

This chapter will begin to show how the financial statements are interrelated through The Accounting Equation. Please be patient as these concepts will be developed gradually over Chapters 3, 4, and 5.

THE EXPANDED ACCOUNTING EQUATION: PART I

Let's begin with The Accounting Equation: Assets = Liabilities + Equity. This is not only The Accounting Equation but it is also the formula for The Balance Sheet. The only difference between the two is that The Balance Sheet is usually in more of a vertical, report-type format (more on that later).

Equity is made up of two main categories as follows:

Equity = Contributed Capital + Retained Earnings

Contributed Capital, also called *Paid-in Capital,* represents the money the owners of a business have directly put into the business in exchange for ownership interest. *Retained Earnings* represents (1) the money the business has earned but, (2) kept within the business. Recall that a synonym for net income was earnings. So, when we're talking about money the business has earned, or earnings, we are talking about the firm's net income.

Second, the earnings belong to the owners of the business. They could take the firm's earnings out of the business and spend it to finance a night on the town. Earnings paid out of a business to its owners are called *Dividends.* Earnings not paid out of the business to its owners are called Retained Earnings.

Why keep earnings within a business? Wouldn't the owners want to take the earnings out of the business and spend them? The answer is a bit complicated, but maybe they are willing to leave some or all of the earnings in the business if they think the business can use these earnings to make even more money in the future. For more than two decades, Microsoft never paid a dividend, yet its stockholders (i.e., its owners) made a lot of money because the company used past earnings to grow, to develop new products, and to cement its position as the dominant software provider for PCs. As it did so, its stock price increased dramatically. Even though the stockholders did not immediately receive their share of the earnings in the form of a dividend, they did enjoy owning a stock whose stock price increased substantially over that same time period.

Here is a formula for Retained Earnings (RE):

RE, Beginning + Net Income – Dividends = RE, Ending

The key points to note in this formula are that (1) net income increases retained earnings, and (2) dividends reduces retained earnings. Don't forget that retained earnings is a subcategory of equity. This allows us to say that net income increases retained earnings, which in turn increases equity. That is, net income increases equity. What if a company lost money, meaning their expenses exceeded their revenue? A loss would decrease retained earnings and decrease equity.

The second key point is that dividends reduce retained earnings as indicated by the minus sign above. This means that earnings paid out to the owners in the form of dividends leaves the company with that much less money to use for growth and new product development in the future. Please don't jump to any conclusions about dividends being bad, but just note that dividends reduce retained earnings, which in turn reduces equity.

What if we substituted the equation for net income into the formula above? Let's abbreviate R for Revenue, EX for Expenses, and D for Dividends to make this more concise:

RE, Beginning + R – EX – D = RE, Ending

What's the point? For now, nothing more than to note that revenues increase retained earnings, which increases equity; expenses reduce retained earnings, which reduces equity.

THE LOTTERY POOL EXAMPLE

Here's a story that might help us with some of these concepts. Let's assume that everyone in a class of 29 students plus the textbook author forms a lottery pool. We have 29 students plus the textbook author so we'll have a total of 30 stockholders, or owners. Since you are all very bright people, you decide to let the textbook author make all the important decisions about what lottery games we should play and what numbers to pick (insert laughter here). We each contribute $1 and in exchange I give you a receipt showing that you have one share of stock in our company. Stock is really just a receipt showing that you have an ownership interest in a venture. We'll have a total of 30 shares of stock and each share will be entitled to one-thirtieth of any winnings.

Let's assume that I buy 30 lottery tickets for $1 each. The tickets are all losers except for one that is worth $90. Our Revenue for the period is $90, our Expenses are $30 representing the cost of the lottery tickets, and our Net Income is ($90 minus $30) $60.

Let's prepare a balance sheet to see where we stand. On the Asset side we have Cash, and on the Liabilities and Equity side we have no liabilities and two components of Equity, the Contributed Capital and the Retained Earnings. This is shown in Table 3.1.

Table 3.1. The Lottery Pool Balance Sheet Before Payment of Dividends

Assets		*Liabilities and Equity*	
Cash	$90	Contributed Capital	$30
		Retained Earnings	60
Total Assets	$90	Total Liabilities and Equity	$90

This is a very simple Balance Sheet representing our Assets on the left-hand side and our Liabilities and Equity on the right-hand side. Please note that The Balance Sheet "balances" in the sense that our total Assets (i.e., $90) equal our total Liabilities plus our total Equity (i.e., $90). We should also note that accountants like to use a single line to indicate they are going to sum a column of numbers and a double underline for the resulting summation.

Now, our group could decide to pay out some of the winnings, which would be called a Dividend. Let's say we decided to pay a Dividend of $0.50 per share, but leave the rest of the winnings in the company so that we can buy even more lottery tickets next week. There are 30 shares so this will mean the company will distribute a total of $15.00 to its owners. This will leave us with the balance sheet shown in Table 3.2.

Table 3.2. The Lottery Pool Balance Sheet After Payment of Dividends

Assets		*Liabilities and Equity*	
Cash	$75	Contributed Capital	$30
		Retained Earnings	45
Total Assets	$75	Total Liabilities and Equity	$75

To recap, the owners put $30 into the business. This is called Contributed Capital. The business had a Net Income of $60 and paid out Dividends of $15, leaving it with Retained Earnings of $45.

We hope this example helps make these terms a bit more concrete. Contributed Capital represents money owners put into the business in exchange for ownership interest. That ownership interest entitles them to a share of any Net Income (i.e., "winnings"). These winnings can either be kept in the business as Retained Earnings or given back to the owners as a reward for risking their money in the company. Please note that a Dividend is typically viewed as coming from the company's Net Income or Earnings, not from the initial amount you put into the lottery pool. If all you do is get your dollar back, it's better than nothing, but it's hardly a reward!

The Chapter 3 review problem 1 repeats this example in a bit more detail and using an approach called transaction analysis. If you are unclear about any of the numbers in this example, you should study this review problem before continuing to Chapter 4.

THE EXPANDED ACCOUNTING EQUATION: PART II

Let's begin again with The Accounting Equation: Assets = Liabilities + Equity. In part II, I'd like to link The Statement of Cash Flows to The Accounting Equation. This will actually be easier than part I. Let's split Assets into two parts:

Assets = Cash + Noncash Assets

Next, let's recall the three categories of cash from The Statement of Cash Flows: Operating, Investing, and Financing. Using these terms, any change in Cash is caused by either an Operating, Investing, or Financing activity.

We will now introduce the Expanded Accounting Equation in Figure 3.1. Please remember that this is not yet supposed to make perfect and complete sense. For now, just try to stick with me and understand why I've created the categories and subcategories under Assets and Equity.

For the sake of brevity in this chapter, we will not include an example using this Expanded Accounting Equation. A detailed example will follow in Chapter 4. However, past experience has indicated that this chapter is a bit long on concepts and a bit short on concrete examples for some readers. Consequently, the Chapter 3 review problem 2 includes an example of how The Expanded Accounting Equation would be used to analyze some common transactions..

SUMMARY

This chapter began with The Accounting Equation from Chapter 2 and developed The Expanded Accounting Equation. The Expanded Accounting Equation shows that The Income Statement is a subcategory of

ASSETS (A)				=	LIABILITIES (L)	+	EQUITY (EQ)			
Cash			Noncash Assets				Contributed Capital	Retained Earnings (RE)		
								Net Income (NI)		Dividends (D)
Operating	Investing	Financing						Revenues (R)	Expenses (EX)	

Figure 3.1. The Expanded Accounting Equation.

Retained Earnings which is a subcategory of Equity. The linkage, then, between The Balance Sheet and The Income Statement is through Retained Earnings. The Income Statement tells us how much we made in a particular time period, while Retained Earnings will tell us how much we have made and kept in the business at any given point in time.

The Expanded Accounting Equation also shows that The Statement of Cash Flows is a subcomponent of Cash. The Statement of Cash Flows helps explain why Cash changes over time using the three categories Operating, Investing, and Financing. On The Balance Sheet, Cash is how much we have on hand at any given point in time.

Chapter 4 is going to go through a series of transactions and apply them to The Expanded Accounting Equation. It is hoped that after doing so, some of these concepts will become a bit clearer. For now, let's view this chapter as laying the foundation for future study.

CHAPTER 3: REVIEW PROBLEM 1

The Lottery Pool Transaction Analysis

1. Each of the 30 people in this class contributes $1 into a lottery pool. In exchange for the money, they each get a receipt showing that they own 1/30th of this "company." The $30 is referred to as Contributed Capital for this "business."
2. The group decides to buy $30 worth of lottery tickets. This is the primary cost of doing business, or Expense, for our company.
3. We learn that we have lots of losers and one winner worth $90. This is the primary source of income, or Revenue, for our business.
4. What is the group's net income (also known as profits, earnings, or the bottom line) from their first round of playing the lottery? The net income is the Revenues of $90 minus the Expenses of $30, or $60 in this example.
5. The group decides to give, or distribute, $0.50 to each owner. This is referred to as a Dividend and represents a distribution of a portion of the company's net income to its owners.
6. What is the group's Retained Earnings? The group's Retained Earnings is now the Net Income of $60 minus the Dividends of $15, or $45. Retained Earnings represents the portion of Net Income that is kept, or retained, in the business.
7. After the above activity, the firm's Balance Sheet consists of one asset, Cash, $75. The firm has no liabilities since we did no borrow any money. The Equity consists of Contributed Capital, $30, and

Retained Earnings, $45. The firm's Liabilities, $0, plus Equity, $75, equal the firm's assets thus making sure The Balance Sheet "balances."

Table 3.3. The Lottery Pool Transaction Analysis Worksheet

	Assets	= *Liabilities* +	*Equity*	
Item	*Cash*		*Contributed Capital*	*Retained Earnings*
1.	+ $30		+ $30	
2.	– $30			– $30
3.	+ $90			+$90
Balances for 4.	+ $90		+$30	+ $60
5.	– $15			– $15
Balances for 6. and 7.	+ $75		+ $30	+ $45

CHAPTER 3: REVIEW PROBLEM 2

A Brief Example Using the Expanded Accounting Equation

This is a story about a new business that is starting with nothing, or zero in the bank and they have no other assets.

1. The company first receives some money from its owners in exchange for stock, or ownership interest, in the company. Let's assume the owners invest $75,000 in the new business.
2. The company then arranges to get a bank loan for an additional $25,000.
3. The business spends $60,000 on equipment for their business. The equipment is expected to last about 5 years and be worth next to nothing at the end of the 5 years.
4. The business generates revenue from sales to customers totaling $125,000 in its first year of business.
5. The business pays day-to-day operating costs (rent on a building, utilities, wages, and a bunch of other smaller items too numerous to mention but not including any of the cost of the equipment) of $95,000.
6. What is the firm's Financing Cash Flow for the year? Answer: +$100,000 cash inflow. What is the firm's Investing Cash Flow for

the year? Answer: – $60,000 cash outflow. What is the firm's Operating Cash Flow for the year? Answer: + $30,000.

7. What is the firm's net income for the year? Answer: Revenues of + $125,000 minus Expenses of – $95,000 equal + $30,000.

Table 3.4. A Brief Example to Illustrate the Expanded Accounting Equation

	ASSETS (A)				= LIABILITIES (L)	+	EQUITY (EQ)		
							Retained Earnings (RE)		
	Cash				Bank	Contributed	Net Income (NI)		
Trans.	Operating	Investing	Financing	Equipment	Loan	Capital	Revenues (R)	Expenses (EX)	Dividends (D)
1.			$75,000			$75,000			
2.			$25,000		$25,000				
3.		($60,000)		$60,000					
4.	$125,000						$125,000		
5.	($95,000)							($95,000)	
Balances for 6 and 7.	$30,000	($60,000)	$100,000	$60,000	$25,000	$75,000	$125,000	($95,000)	

CHAPTER 4

BASIC TRANSACTION ANALYSIS

INTRODUCTION

Chapter 3 began with The Accounting Equation and ended with The Expanded Accounting Equation. The Expanded Accounting Equation illustrates that The Income Statement is linked to The Balance Sheet through a new component of Equity called Retained Earnings. The Income Statement reports the amount of Revenues, Expenses, and Net Income for a period of time (e.g., 1 year) and The Balance Sheet reports the amount of Assets, Liabilities and Equity at a certain point in time (e.g., beginning of year, end of year).

The Expanded Accounting Equation also illustrates that The Statement of Cash Flows is linked to The Balance Sheet through the asset Cash. The Statement of Cash Flows shows the cash inflows and cash outflows for a certain period of time (e.g., 1 year) categorized into Operating, Investing, and Financing cash flows. The Balance Sheet reports the amount of cash on hand at a particular point in time (e.g., beginning of year or end of year).

This chapter introduces the concept of transaction analysis. Transaction analysis is determining how economic events affect The Expanded Accounting Equation.

Financial Accounting: A Course for All Majors, pp. 25–32

TRANSACTION ANALYSIS

Assume you've acquired a good bit of expertise within your field of study and have been approached by several persons to give them advice and help. After discovering that you have some knowledge that is quite valuable to others, you decide to start your own consulting business. The following transactions relate to your new business.

This is our introduction to transaction analysis. You need to take an *active role* in this exercise. Print out the workpaper in Table 4.1 and fill in the appropriate blanks as we go through each transaction below.

The transactions below are related to your new business. Following each transaction we have inserted an explanation of how the transaction affected The Expanded Accounting Equation. This is a difficult, and perhaps tedious, assignment so follow along closely and record the answers on the workpaper as we move through the explanations.

Before we begin, we need to make a very important point. *The Accounting Equation as well as The Expanded Accounting Equation must always remain in balance.* That is, Assets must always equal Liabilities plus Equity. In short, *this means that every economic transaction that is recorded will affect at least two items in the equation.* Mathematically you simply cannot change one element in an equation and retain equality for the overall equation. In accounting, we refer to this as *double-entry accounting.*

1. January 1, 20X1. You form a corporation and put all the available cash you have, $15,000, into the business to provide the money to get it started. In exchange for the money, you receive ownership interest, or "stock," in the new legal entity.

Please keep in mind throughout this exercise that we are recording these transactions from the perspective of the new business, not its owner. For the new business, transaction 1 represents a Financing Cash Inflow and Contributed Capital. On our workpaper, we will show a +15,000 in the Financing Cash Flow column and another +15,000 in the Contributed Capital column.

2. January 1, 20X1. Since you have put some of your own money into the new business you are able to convince your dear Aunt Josephine to loan you some additional money needed for start-up costs. She loans you $5,000 (with no interest), with repayment to be made on December 31, 20X1.

Table 4.1. Chapter 4 Transaction Analysis Workpaper

	ASSETS (A)					=	LIABILITIES (L)		+	EQUITY (EQ)			
											Retained Earnings (RE)		
	Cash			Equipment			Note			Contributed	Net Income (NI)		
Trans.	Operating	Investing	Financing				Payable			Capital	Revenues (R)	Expenses (EX)	Dividends (D)
1.													
2.													
3.													
4.													
5.													
6.													
7.													
8.													
9.													
10.													
Totals													

Remember that there are two, primary ways to finance a new venture, debt or equity. Transaction 1 is an example of using equity to finance a new business; transaction 2 is an example of using debt as a means of financing. On your workpaper, Financing Cash Flows will increase by +5,000. Transaction 2 must be repaid so this is debt, or a Liability. I've created a column in the workpaper for Note Payable to represent this liability. Record a +5,000 there now to show that we have incurred a $5,000 debt by borrowing this money from Aunt Josephine.

Let's pause for a moment here to ask several questions. What is your *debt ratio?* The debt ratio is your total liabilities divided by your total assets. A company's *capital structure* refers to the relative amounts of debt and equity they use to finance their assets. In our case, our total liabilities are $5,000 and our total assets are $20,000, so our debt ratio is ($5,000 / $20,000) one-fourth, or 25%. This simply means that we have financed 25% of our total assets with borrowed money, or debt.

3. January 1, 20X1. You sign an agreement to rent an office for $500 per month, or $6,000 per year. This would probably result in a total of 12 transactions, or entries, throughout the year. For our purposes, we will just make one entry to summarize this cost for the entire year.

This is our first example of a day-to-day operating cost. On your workpaper we will record an Operating Cash Outflow of – 6,000 (minus because it is a cash payment, or outflow) and an Expense of – 6,000. Why is the Expense recorded as a minus? Expenses reduce Net Income, Expenses reduce Retained Earnings, and Expenses reduce Equity so we illustrate them mathematically on the workpaper with a minus sign. This leads to the odd, but correct, result that when you *increase* Expenses you are *decreasing* Net Income, Retained Earnings, and Equity.

4. You buy some equipment for the office (computers, printers, etc.) at a total cash cost of $4,500. You hope this equipment will last three years before you have to replace it.

This is our first example of an Investing-type activity for our business. An Investing-type activity in this case means buying an asset with a relatively long life, where "relatively long life" means more than one year. On your workpaper, record an Investing Cash Outflow for – 4,500. What did the business get in exchange for this Cash? It received an asset we will label Equipment. One asset, Cash, decreases when we pay for the item, while another asset, Equipment, increases to represent that we now have Equipment that cost us $4,500. Your workpaper should reflect – 4,500 Investing Cash Outflow and a + 4,500 in the Equipment column.

There are several points to make here. First, it is sometimes difficult to distinguish between Investing and Financing activities. Remember that we are doing this from the perspective of the new business. Transactions 1 and 2 are ways the new business obtained its initial money to begin. For the business, these are Financing activities. In transaction 4, the business is using some of its money to acquire a long-term asset, which is our definition of an Investing activity.

Second, compare transaction 3 and 4. Both transactions involve an outflow of cash but in 3 we recorded an Expense while in 4 we recorded an Asset, Equipment. Why? In transaction 3 we were paying the monthly rent on the office. All we are getting is the monthly usage of the office. An Expense is something that has no more future value. At the end of the rental period, the business has no ownership interest in the office space. In contrast, in transaction 4 we are buying the Equipment. An Asset is something that has future value and we expect the Equipment to provide benefits to our business for up to three years after which we might be able to get a few dollars back by selling it to someone else. The point is we have ownership of the equipment so it is an Asset to us.

Finally, note in transaction 4 that we can maintain the equality of our equation by recording both affects on the same side of the equals sign. That is, in transaction 1, 2, and 3, we recorded one affect on the left-hand side of the equals sign (the Asset side) and the other on the right-hand side of the equals sign (the Liabilities and Equity side). In transaction 4 we decreased one Asset, Cash, but increased another Asset, Equipment. The net affect is that our equation still balances—Assets equal Liabilities plus Equity.

5. During your first year of business the cash received from customers in exchange for consulting advice totals $75,000.

This is our first example of a Revenue transaction. The primary way a business earns Revenue is by providing a good or service to its customers. On your workpaper, record + 75,000 as an Operating Cash Inflow and + 75,000 in the Revenue column.

6. You are paid a monthly salary of $2,500 per month, or $30,000 per year. Just make one entry to summarize payment for the entire year.

Remember that we are recording these transactions from the perspective of the business. From this perspective, you are not only the owner, but an indispensable employee of the business and the business can pay you a reasonable salary for your services. In fact, if you were not employed the business would, in theory, have to hire someone else with equal capabilities. On your workpaper, record an Operating Cash Outflow of – 30,000 and an Expense for – 30,000.

> 7. You hire an office manager to take care of the things that a busy consultant can not do, like deposit checks from customers, pay the bills, answer the phone, etc. His salary is $1,500 per month, or $18,000 per year. Just make one entry to summarize payment for the entire year.

Transaction 6 and 7 are similar in that they both represent what we might call Salary or Wages Expense. Record an Operating Cash Outflow of – 18,000 and an Expense for – 18,000.

> 8. Utilities on the office cost you about $600 per month, or $7,200 per year. Just make one entry for the entire year.

Transaction 8 is an example of another day-to-day operating cost of the business, utilities. Record an Operating Cash Outflow of – 7,200 and an Expense for – 7,200.

> 9. Additional day-to-day costs of doing business total $10,000 for the year.

Transaction 9 is what happens when you make up a classroom example and when you're done it seems like the business was too profitable, especially since this is only its first year of business and most new businesses lose money in the beginning! We must have forgotten some other expenses, hence the reason for transaction 9. Record an Operating Cash Outflow of – 10,000 and an Expense for – 10,000.

> 10. At the end of the year you repay the note to Aunt Josephine.

Let's go back and look at how we recorded transaction 2 for a moment. When we borrowed the money from our dear Auntie, we recorded a Financing Cash Inflow of + 5,000 and a Note Payable of + 5,000. Since we are now repaying this debt, let's simply do the opposite. Record a minus 5,000 Financing Cash Outflow and reduce the Note Payable by 5,000 to show that we have now repaid the loan and no longer have a Note Payable to Aunt Josephine.

Table 4.2. Chapter 4 Completed Transaction Analysis Workpaper

	ASSETS (A)					=	LIABILITIES (L)		+	EQUITY (EQ)			
											Retained Earnings (RE)		
	Cash			Equipment			Note			Contributed	Net Income (NI)		
Trans.	Operating	Investing	Financing				Payable			Capital	Revenues (R)	Expenses (EX)	Dividends (D)
1.			$15,000							$15,000			
2.			$5,000				$5,000						
3.	($6,000)											($6,000)	
4.		($4,500)		$4,500									
5.	$75,000										$75,000		
6.	($30,000)											($30,000)	
7.	($18,000)											($18,000)	
8.	($7,200)											($7,200)	
9.	($10,000)											($10,000)	
10.			($5,000)				($5,000)						
Totals	$3,800	($4,500)	$15,000	$4,500			$0			$15,000	$75,000	($71,200)	

Your last assignment in this chapter is to total each column on your workpaper paying careful attention to add the pluses and subtract the minuses. Record the column total on the last line of each column. Table 4.2 shows the completed workpaper so you may check your work but you must attempt this yourself first to get the most value out of this chapter.

SUMMARY

This is our first exposure to transaction analysis. It is a potentially confusing subject and we would not expect every transaction to make sense to every person the first time. In Chapter 5 we will see the financial statements that go along with this example. Save your workpaper from this chapter so that we can trace these results through from the transactions (our inputs) to the financial statements (our outputs).

CHAPTER 5

FINANCIAL STATEMENT INTERRELATIONSHIPS

INTRODUCTION

Chapter 4 introduced transaction analysis and illustrated the concept with 10 transactions from a fictional new business. This chapter continues with that example so you will need to have your workpaper from Chapter 4 available as you work through this material.

FINANCIAL STATEMENT INTERRELATIONSHIPS

This chapter is going to adopt the old adage that a picture is worth a thousand words. Or, in this case, an illustration is worth a thousand words. Figure 5.1 illustrates how the three major financial statements are connected, or interrelated to use a fancier term. It should be read from left to right. **Please note that this first illustration does not go along with your exercise from Chapter 4.**

On the left-hand side of the illustration, dated January 1, 20X1, is the balance sheet for Example Company at the beginning of the year. All amounts in this example are assumed and may be taken as givens. Again, this illustration is not related to your workpaper from Chapter 4.

Financial Accounting: A Course for All Majors, pp. 33–40

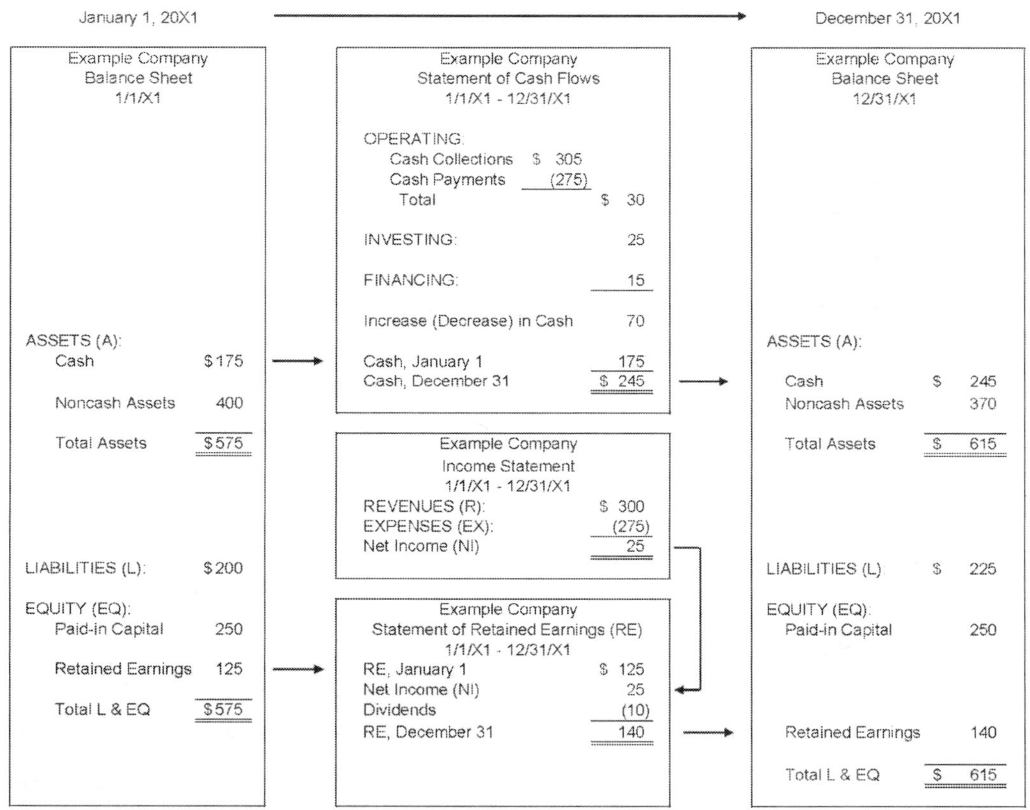

Figure 5.1. Financial Statement Overview and Key Linkages.

On the right-hand side is the balance sheet for Example Company at the end of the year, December 31, 20X1. A balance sheet always show what you have (Assets), what you owe (Liabilities) and what you're worth (Equity) at a specific point in time. It is a *snapshot of your financial position on a specific date.*

Now, what a balance sheet does not tell you about is any activity that took place during a period of time. In this illustration, the middle column includes some reports that summarize what took place during the year. Again, *all the reports in the middle column are summarizing events that took place during a period of time.* These reports are analogous to a movie, while the balance sheet is analogous to a single snapshot at a point in time.

In the middle column, top box, is The Statement of Cash Flows. Note that if you add the Operating Cash Flows of $30 plus the Investing Cash Flows of $25 plus the Financing Cash Flows of $15, you get the Increase in Cash for the year of $70. Add this Increase in Cash of $70 to the beginning Cash balance of $175, and you get the ending Cash balance of $245. Note the Cash balance at any given date is reported on The Balance Sheet. If you want to know why the Cash balance changed over time, say from $175 at the beginning of this year to $245 at the end of this year, then you need to look at The Statement of Cash Flows. It will tell you, in summary form, why your cash changed as it did over time.

In the middle column, middle box, is The Income Statement with the now familiar items Revenues, Expenses and Net Income. Example Company was profitable during 20X1 since it had a Net Income of $25.

What was Example Company's *profit margin?* Profit margin is defined as Net Income divided by Revenue, or ($25 / $300) .0833. In percentage terms their profit margin is 8.33%, meaning that for every $1 of Revenue they are making a bottom line profit of 8.33 cents. This may not seem like much, but this is actually a pretty healthy profit margin. Although some businesses do better than this, many have smaller profit margins but are still successful.

In the middle column, bottom box, is the statement of retained earnings. Perhaps we should capitalize this statement but to me it is not one of the major financial statements. It is a report, a financial statement, true, but not one of "the big three." The statement of retained earnings shows that we started the year with $125 in Retained Earnings. Recall that Retained Earnings is all the Net Income ever earned by the business since its inception and kept within the business. That is, not paid out to its owners as Dividends. The arrow from The Income Statement shows that Net Income increases, or adds to, Retained Earnings. Dividends decrease, or take away from, Retained Earnings. The net result is that Example Company ended the year with Retained Earnings of $140. The statement of retained earnings shows what caused Retained Earnings to change over time, while each balance sheet merely shows the amount of Retained Earnings at a specific point in time.

Figure 5.2 shows the financial statements that go along with the exercise from Chapter 4. Note that the balance sheet on the left-hand side is basically blank in this example because we assumed this was a new business. The business did not exist, on January 1, 20X1, so its balance sheet was basically a blank sheet of paper.

During the year the business generated $3,800 Operating Cash Inflow and $15,000 Financing Cash Inflow, but used $4,500 for an Investing Cash Outflow (equipment purchase). The net result is that the company's Cash increased by $14,300 during 20X1. Since they started the year with zero Cash, they ended the year with $14,300 Cash as shown at the bottom of The Statement of Cash Flows and on The Balance Sheet on the right-hand side of the illustration.

Compare your Chapter 4 workpaper notes to this illustration. You should note that the column totals from your workpaper correspond to what is reported on these financial statements. In a sense, the financial statements are just a different way to report, or present, the information from the workpaper.

The Income Statements shows that we have Revenue of $75,000, Expenses of $71,200, and Net Income of $3,800 for the year. Our profit margin was [($3,800 / $75,000) * 100] 5.07% (rounded).

We started the year with nothing so Retained Earnings was zero. Our Net Income adds to Retained Earnings and Dividends, had there been any, would have reduced Retained Earnings. Since the business did not choose to pay any Dividends we end the year with $3,800 in Retained Earnings.

AN IMPORTANT TASK FOR THIS CHAPTER

To test your understanding of the financial statement overviews and key linkages from this chapter two additional examples are provided in Figures 5.3 and 5.4. As you review these problems start thinking about whether you understand the financial statement interrelationships well enough that you could solve for missing values in the financial statements.

TRANSACTION ANALYSIS REVIEW FOR CHAPTERS 1–5

Transaction analysis is often the most difficult task covered in Chapters 1–5. A quick review is provided in Table 5.1. This illustration summarizes the seven key transactions that we have covered to this point in the book.

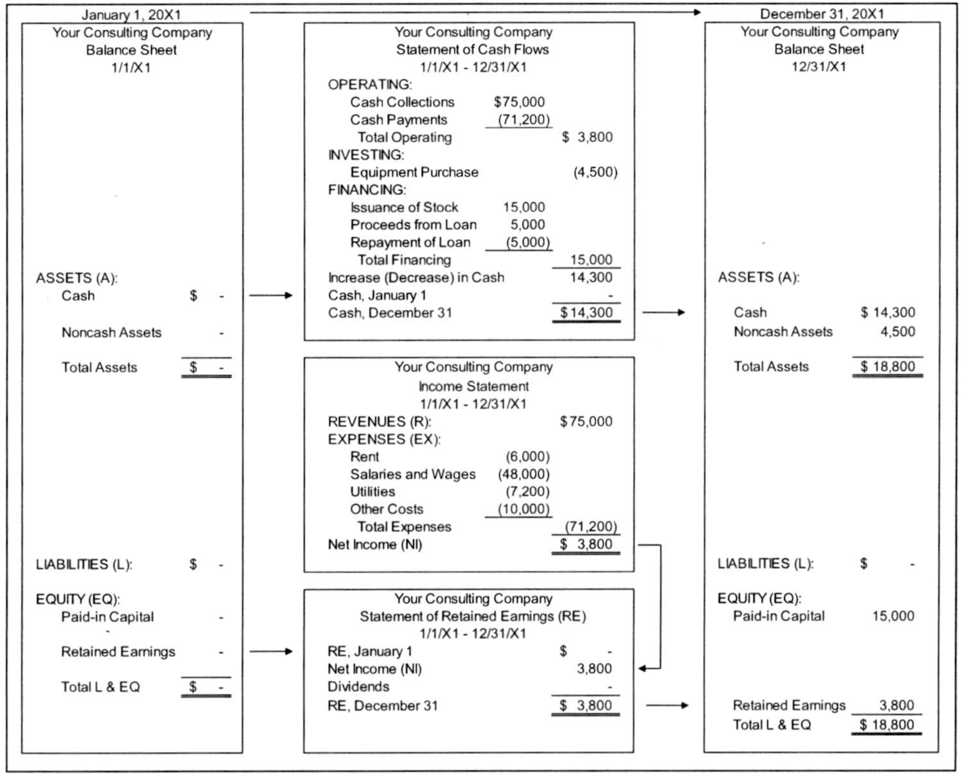

Figure 5.2. Financial Statement Overview and Key Linkages to Accompany Chapter 4 Example.

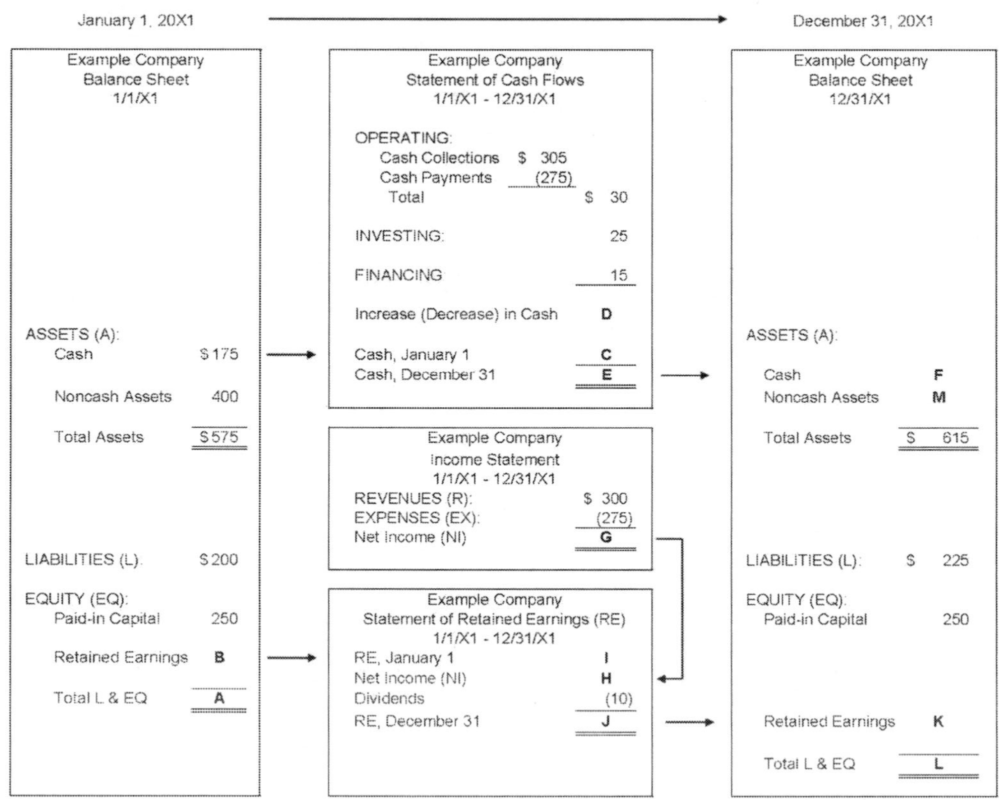

Figure 5.3. Financial Statement Interrelationships With Missing Values— Example 1.

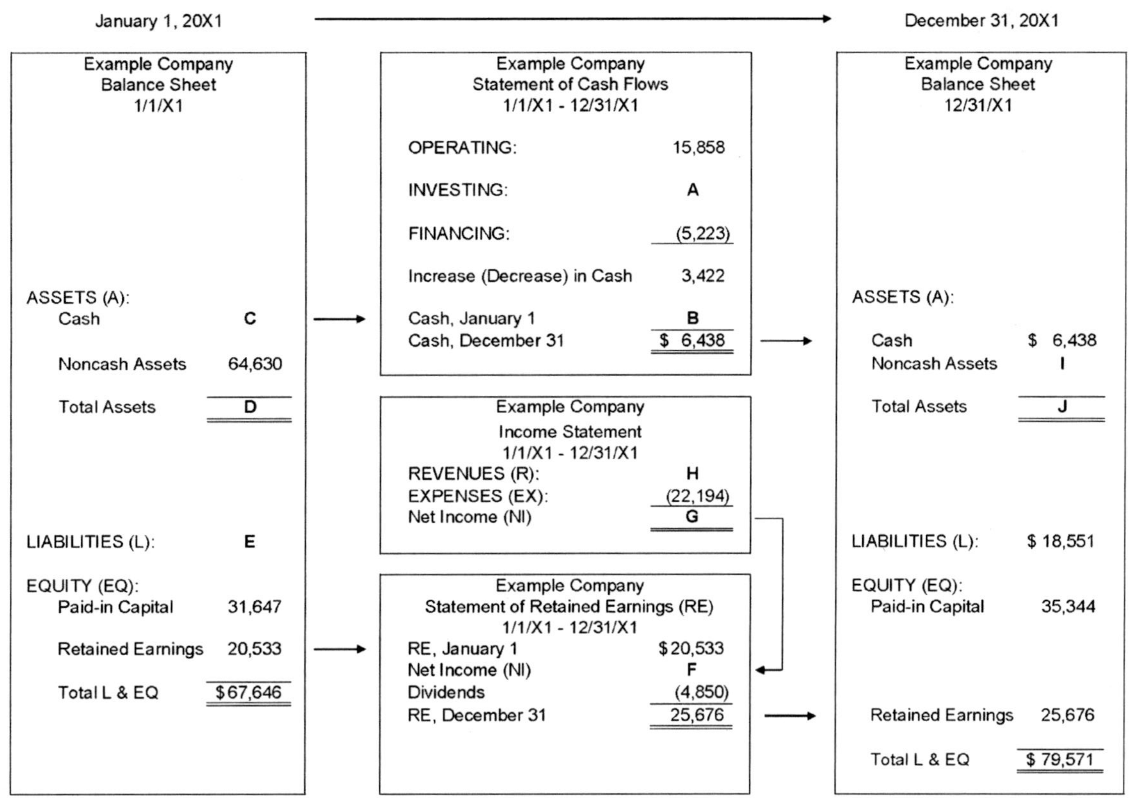

Figure 5.4. Financial Statement Interrelationships With Missing Values—Example 2.

SUMMARY

The illustrations in this chapter provide the reader with an overall view of the content in the financial statements, and how the three, major financial statements are linked to each other.

Chapter 1 began this course with an overview of the accounting profession. Chapter 2 introduced Financial Accounting and the three, major financial statements. Chapter 3 introduced The Expanded Accounting Equation, Chapter 4 provided an application of this equation, and Chapter 5 provides the related set of financial statements for this exercise.

We have already covered a lot of difficult material in this course. Our book is designed for an exam after Chapters 1–5 so that you will stop, focus, and make sure you have mastered this material before we move on to new topics. For the most part, this course is cumulative in the sense that you really need to understand prior chapters to do well in future chapters.

Table 5.1. Transaction Analysis Review for Chapters 1–5

	ASSETS (A)				= LIABILITIES (L)	+ EQUITY (EQ)			
	Cash						Retained Earnings (RE)		
	Operating	Investing	Financing	Equipment	Notes Payable	Contributed Capital	Revenue (R)	Expense (EX)	Dividends (D)
1. Issuing, or selling, stock in exchange for cash.			+			+			
2. Borrowing money.			+		+				
3. Repaying borrowed money (ignore interest for now).			-		-				
4. Buying a long-term asset (e.g., equipment) with cash.		-		+					
5. Making cash sales to customers.	+						+		
6. Paying cash for day-to-day costs of doing business (not on account but paid as incurred).	-							-	
7. Distributing some of the profits to the owners.			-						-

CHAPTER 6

THE ACCRUAL BASIS OF ACCOUNTING

INTRODUCTION

Chapter 4 introduced the concept of transaction analysis. This chapter will expand on transaction analysis, but with the addition of several, new concepts. We will begin with the concept of the *basis of accounting.*

BASIS OF ACCOUNTING

Basis of accounting refers to when revenues and expenses are recorded, or recognized in our financial records. There are two, primary choices with respect to basis of accounting. One is called *cash basis of accounting* and the other is called *accrual basis of accounting*.

With the cash basis of accounting, revenues are recognized when you receive the cash payment from a customer in exchange for providing them a good or service; expenses are recognized when you pay for a good or service you have purchased. The name, cash basis, stems from the fact that revenue is not recognized unless you have received cash and expenses are not recognized until you have paid cash. In filing our personal income tax returns (not the focus of this course) most of us probably

Financial Accounting: A Course for All Majors, pp. 43–49

use the cash basis of accounting. (we only mention this because sometimes students will say, "but that's not how it works on my tax return" and they are correct, but that's because the tax return may require a different basis of accounting than the one about to be introduced here.)

The accrual basis of accounting is what we will use in this course. With the accrual basis of accounting, revenues are recognized when you have earned them, and expenses are recognized when they have been incurred. You might want to pause here and reread the preceding sentence.

With accrual basis accounting, revenues are recognized when you have earned them, which may or may not be the same time period that you receive the cash. For example, if you go to work today, will you get a pay check at the end of your shift? Unless today just happens to be a scheduled pay day, the answer is no. However, don't you feel like you have earned payment for your work today? By going to work and providing a service for your employer you have earned revenue even though you will not receive payment until the next pay day.

With accrual basis accounting, expenses are recognized when you have incurred them even though you may not have paid the bill yet. For some reason, most of us can identify with the expense side of this easier than with the revenue part of this discussion! For example, if you go out to dinner this evening and pay the bill with a credit card, have you incurred an expense? Under accrual basis accounting the answer is yes, even though you have not yet paid the bill. You incurred the expense by eating the meal and enjoying the atmosphere with family or friends. And, while you can savor the memories, the meal is an expense, not an asset, because once eaten it is gone forever.

We will now proceed directly to an example using the accrual basis of accounting.

TRANSACTION ANALYSIS WITH ACCRUAL BASIS ACCOUNTING

Before we begin this illustration of accrual basis accounting, let's do the same thing we did in Chapter 4 with transaction analysis. Print out the workpaper in Table 6.1 and get ready to follow along. Note that on this workpaper we only have one column for Cash, and it is the Operating Cash Flows category. As it turns out Investing and Financing Cash Flows are not affected much by the basis of accounting.

1. On May 1, 20X1, the company paid cash for $1,800 of supplies and recorded the supplies as an asset.

Table 6.1. Chapter 6 Transaction Analysis Workpaper

	ASSETS (A)					=	LIABILITIES (L)		+	EQUITY (EQ)			
											Retained Earnings (RE)		
	Cash										Net Income (NI)		
Trans.	Operating	Accounts Receivable	Office Supplies	Prepaid Insurance			Unearned Revenue	Accounts Payable		Contributed Capital	Revenues (R)	Expenses (EX)	Dividends (D)
1													
2													
3													
4													
5													
6													
7													
8													
Subtotal													

Cash is clearly decreased here since it says you "paid" cash, but what did we get in exchange? If we got something with no future value (e.g., the meal in my earlier example) then we would record an Expense. In this case we got something that we will keep and presumably use in the future, supplies. Something that is going to be used up in the future, but still have value today, is an Asset. We will record this transaction by decreasing one asset, Cash, and increasing another asset, Supplies.

2. On June 15, 20X1, the company billed customers for services that had been provided, $10,000.

The term "billed" here means that our company has provided the customer a good or service, has sent the customer a bill, but has not yet received payment from the customer for this work. Since we are using accrual basis accounting now, how should we record this transaction? Have we earned the Revenue? Using accrual basis accounting we will answer yes because we have done what is required of us to be entitled to receive payment from the customer now or in the future. We will record an increase to Revenue, but we cannot record an increase to Cash because we have not been paid yet. Let's create a new Asset called *Accounts Receivable,* or sometimes just *Receivables,* to reflect the amount of goods or services provided to customers but for which we have not yet received payment.

To recap, we will increase Revenue and increase an Asset called Accounts Receivable for this transaction. Please note that in doing so we are making an assumption that we will ultimately get paid for our work. This assumption is the reason we can record an Asset, Accounts Receivable. An Asset is something that has future value and the future value of the Accounts Receivable is the Cash that we expect to receive from our customer when she finally pays her bill.

3. On August 1, 20X1, the company received $24,000 from a customer. This amount is an advance payment for services to be provided by the company evenly over the next 6 months.

This seems like an odd transaction since the company is being paid in advance for services that it will provide in the future. Although this is a nice arrangement for the company, it may not seem very practical, or realistic. However, think about what many of us do when buying gift cards from a retailer. We pay the retailer today, and in exchange we expect them to honor the gift card in the future. Prepaid cell phone plans are similar in that the business receives cash before earning revenue by providing the service. The point is, businesses do sometimes get paid in advance for their goods or services.

Ok, how to record this transaction? Let's do the easy part first and record an increase to Operating Cash Flow since we "received" cash. Now, have we earned revenue? No, because we have not yet provided the service. What if we never provided the service? Wouldn't we owe the customer a refund? By accepting the cash, the company in this case has an obligation, or Liability, to the customer to either provide the service in the future or refund the customer's money. We are going to create a new Liability called *Unearned Revenue* to reflect amounts we have received but for which we have not yet provided the good or service.

4. On September 1, 20X1, the company received its annual bill for property insurance totaling $3,600, for the period September 1, 2006, through August 31, 2007. To avoid service fees, they decided to pay the entire annual premium and to record the amount as an asset.

The company is paying a bill here so reduce Operating Cash Flows. The company is getting insurance coverage in exchange for this payment. The insurance coverage is for the future so we will argue that the company is getting an Asset in exchange for this payment. The future benefit to justify recording an Asset is the insurance coverage we are entitled to receive over the next 12 months. We will call this asset *Prepaid Insurance.* It belongs to a class of assets sometimes loosely referred to as "Prepaids" as they represent things that we have paid for in advance and will probably use up in the future.

5. On September 10, 20X1, the company finally received a partial payment of $6,000 from the customers billed on June 15.

In this transaction we are receiving payment from the customers in transaction 2. Increase Operating Cash Flow by $6,000 since it says we "received" payment. Let's pause for a moment here and think about what the customer owes us before and after this payment. Before this payment they owed us $10,000 from transaction 2; after the payment they will only owe us the balance of $10,000 minus the $6,000 payment, or $4,000. How can we show this on our records? Let's reduce Accounts Receivable by the amount paid, $6,000.

To recap, we will increase one Asset, Operating Cash Flow, and decrease another Asset, Accounts Receivable. After doing so, the balance in the Accounts Receivable column, $4,000, represents the amount the customer still owes us from the work done in transaction 2.

6. On October 1, 20X1, the company received a bill for advertisements that had already run in the local media, $1,500. The bill will be paid later.

The ads had "already run in the local media" so will treat this as if we will not be getting any additional future benefits from this item. A cost that we have incurred for which we will not receive any additional future benefits is an Expense. Let's record an Expense by showing a negative amount in the Expense column. Since we have not paid the bill yet we will need to record a Liability for this item. This Liability will be called an *Accounts Payable,* sometimes loosely referred to simply as *Payables.*

Don't get sidetracked here, but doesn't it upset you when we record an Expense with a negative amount? At the very least it might be confusing. Expenses reduce Equity so we record them with negative amounts, or minus signs. This leads to the confusing issue of recording an increase in Expenses with a negative amount; that is, to record an increase in Expenses we nevertheless show it on our books as a negative item.

7. On November 15, 20X1, the company received the remaining amount due from the customers billed on June 15.

What is the remaining balance still due from customers in transaction 2? We also call this the customer's *account balance.* On your workpaper it is the balance shown in the Accounts Receivable column, $10,000 originally billed in transaction 2 minus $6,000 paid in transaction 5.

8. On November 20, 2006, the company paid the advertising bill.

The good news is we're just about done with this chapter. The advertising bill was received in transaction 6 at which time we recorded the Expense and the associated Payable. Now we are paying the bill. Reduce Operating Cash Flow and reduce Accounts Payable by the same amount, $1,500.

Before we stop, determine the balance in each column and let's quickly summarize the results of these eight transactions. Operating Cash Flows increased by a total amount of $27,100, Accounts Receivable ends with a balance of $0 since customers have paid us in full, while Office Supplies and Prepaid Insurance still have their original amounts of $1,800 and $3,600, respectively. One can't help but wonder whether we still have the original amounts of supplies and insurance but that is the topic for Chapter 7.

On the Liability side, Accounts Payable is $0 since we have paid the advertising bill in full, but Unearned Revenue still has a balance of $24,000. We wonder if we have provided any of this service by the end of the year, but we will defer that until chapter 7. Finally, Revenues total $10,000 and Expenses only $1,500 for this brief example of accrual basis accounting.

SUMMARY

This chapter has introduced the accrual basis of accounting and the concept that one can record Revenue before cash is received, and record Expense before cash is paid. Please note the reverse is also true. Under accrual basis accounting, you may receive cash, but not record Revenue if you have not yet earned it. You may also pay cash, but not record an Expense if you have not yet consumed or used up the item in question.

Table 6.2 contains the solution file for this example so that you can verify your workpaper solution is correct. Chapter 7 will continue this example so keep your workpaper for that chapter.

Table 6.2. Chapter 6 Completed Transaction Analysis Workpaper

	ASSETS (A)					= LIABILITIES (L)		+ EQUITY (EQ)			
									Retained Earnings (RE)		
	Cash								Net Income (NI)		
Trans.	Operating	Accounts Receivable	Office Supplies	Prepaid Insurance		Unearned Revenue	Accounts Payable	Contributed Capital	Revenues (R)	Expenses (EX)	Dividends (D)
1	($1,800)		$1,800								
2		$10,000							$10,000		
3	$24,000					$24,000					
4	($3,600)			$3,600							
5	$6,000	($6,000)									
6							$1,500			($1,500)	
7	$4,000	($4,000)									
8	($1,500)						($1,500)				
Subtotal	$27,100	$0	$1,800	$3,600		$24,000	$0		$10,000	($1,500)	

CHAPTER 7

ACCRUALS AND DEFERRALS

INTRODUCTION

Chapter 6 introduced the idea of the basis of accounting. Using the accrual basis of accounting Revenues are recognized when earned, and Expenses are recognized when incurred. We will continue with this discussion in Chapter 7.

ACCRUALS AND DEFERRALS

Perhaps the accrual basis of accounting should be called the "accrual and deferral basis of accounting" because these two terms, accrual and deferral, are the foundation for this basis of accounting. These terms are defined by comparing when cash is received or paid versus when Revenue or Expense is recognized.

Accruals and deferrals are all about *differences in timing* between when Revenue or Expense should be recognized under the accrual basis of accounting and when cash is actually received or paid. We will begin our discussion with accruals followed by deferrals.

Financial Accounting: A Course for All Majors, pp. 51–56

ACCRUALS

Accrued revenues are when we earn revenue before receiving the cash payment:

Accrued Revenues: Revenue Earned Now → Cash Received Later

A personal example is when you go to work each day and earn revenue but do not get your pay check until the next pay day. What justifies recording Revenue before we receive the cash? Well, you provided services to your employer and certainly expect to get paid for those services. The fact that, as a matter of practicality and convenience, employers do not pay every day does not mean you did not earn Revenue by going to work today. It does mean there is a *difference in timing* between when you do the work and when you receive payment for the work.

For a business, accrued revenue results when a good or service is provided before payment is received from the customer. The most common example involves Accounts Receivable. When a good or service is provided, Accounts Receivable and Revenue are both increased to record the transaction. What happens when payment is later received? Operating Cash Flow is increased and Accounts Receivable is decreased to record the collection of the receivable.

In this context, accrue means to record early, or bring forward, so when we say we are "accruing" Revenue it means we are recording Revenues when earned even though the related cash receipt will not follow until later.

Accrued expenses are when we incur an expense before paying the bill:

Accrued Expenses: Expense Incurred Now → Cash Paid Later

This occurs to us when we "charge now and pay later" using a credit card. We typically incur an Expense when we charge an item on our credit card, but we do not pay for the item until later.

For a business, accrued expenses result when their vendors allow them to buy something today and pay for it later. The accrual basis of accounting says that you can not ignore the Expense just because you have not paid for it; in fact, to get a realistic picture of all your Expenses you need to recognize accrued expenses even though you have not yet paid the bill.

An Accrued Expense results when something with no future value is acquired, consumed, or used up before it is paid for. When the cost is incurred, Accounts Payable is increased to record the Liability, and Equity is reduced by recording an Expense. When the bill is later paid, Operating Cash Flow is reduced and the Account Payable is also reduced to reflect the payment of the bill.

Again, accrue means to record early, or bring forward. In the context of an accrued expense when we say we are "accruing" Expenses it means we are recording Expenses when incurred even though the related cash payment will not be made until later.

DEFERRALS

Deferred revenues are when we receive cash today, but do not earn it until later. For many individuals this does not happen very often so it should not be surprising that it is a difficult concept to grasp.

Deferred Revenues:
Cash Received Now → Revenue Earned Later

A common example of deferred revenue is gift cards. When a retailer sells a gift card, they receive cash today, but they do not earn the Revenue until later when they honor the gift card. The accrual basis of accounting dictates that the retailer not recognize the Revenue until that later date when they have provided the good or service in exchange for the gift card. Note that we are once again talking about *timing differences.* In this case there is a timing difference between when the retailer receives cash and when she provides the related good or service.

Deferred Revenue is also referred to as *Unearned Revenue.* It results when cash is received as payment in advance for goods or services to be provided in the future. When the advance payment is received, Operating Cash Flow is increased and a liability, Unearned Revenue, is increased to record the obligation we have to provide the good or service in the future (or refund the customer's money). When the good or service is later provided, we reduce the Liability called Unearned Revenue to show that we have satisfied our obligation to the customer and we increase Revenue since we have now earned the right to keep the advance payment.

Deferred expenses are when we pay for something today but do not incur the related expense until later:

Deferred Expenses:
Cash Paid Now → Expense Incurred Later

At a personal level, this occurs when you pay for auto or house insurance in advance. Other personal examples include prepaid cell phone service plans, prepaid download services for your favorite music or video, and prepaid credit cards. In all cases, when you initially pay for the item you are acquiring an Asset (future good or service) that will become an Expense when it is consumed or used up in the future. This leads to a very common definition: *an Asset that is used up and no longer has any future value is an Expense.*

Deferred Expenses are also referred to as *Prepaid Expenses,* or simply *Prepaids.* These are items where we pay for something before we use it up, consume it, or it expires. When we pay for the item, Operating Cash Flow is decreased and an Asset, Prepaid ______ (fill in the blank with whatever is being acquired), is increased. Later when the Asset is used up, consumed, or expires we reduce the Asset and reduce Equity by recording an Expense.

CHAPTER 6 TRANSACTIONS REVISITED

At this point, please go back to Table 6.2 and review transactions 1 through 8. For each transaction, classify it as an accrued revenue, accrued expense, deferred revenue, or deferred expense. If a transaction is related to another transaction (e.g., transactions 2, 5, and 7) then all of them will have the same answer. The answers to this short exercise appear at the end of this chapter.

TRANSACTION ANALYSIS FOR ACCRUALS AND DEFERRALS

Table 7.1 summarizes the affects of accruals and deferrals on the accounting transaction. Many of the conceptual problems students have in later chapters, and accounting courses, can be traced back to a fundamental failure to grasp the concepts of accruals and deferrals. We highly recommend you not only memorize the following table, but also do you very best to understand the affects of each transaction on the accounting equation.

CHAPTER 6 TRANSACTIONS REVISITED—SOLUTION

Classify each of the transactions in Chapter 6 as either an accrued revenue, accrued expense, deferred revenue, or deferred expense.

Table 7.1. Transaction Analysis With Accruals and Deferrals

Transaction Type	*Initial Transaction*	*Subsequent Transaction*
Accrued Revenue	+ Receivable, + Equity (Revenue)**	– Receivable, + Operating Cash Flow
Accrued Expense	+ Payable, – Equity (Expense)**	– Payable, – Operating Cash Flow
Deferred Revenue	+ Operating Cash Flow, + Unearned Revenue	– Unearned Revenue, + Equity (Revenue) ^ ^
Deferred Expense	– Operating Cash Flow, + Asset (Prepaid Item)	– Asset, – Equity (Expense) ^ ^

+ indicates an item is increased, – indicates an item is decreased

** Note that Revenue is recorded once when it is first earned, but not again when payment is received; expense is recorded once when it is incurred, but not again when the bill is paid

^ ^ Note that Revenue is not recorded until it is earned; Expense is not recorded until the item is used up, consumed, or expires.

- Transaction 1 is a deferred expense because we paid for something today, but we will not use it up until later.
- Transaction 2 is an accrued revenue because we provided the good or service today, but we will not receive payment until later.
- Transaction 3 is a deferred revenue because we are receiving cash today, but we will not earn the revenue until later.
- Transaction 4 is a deferred expense because we are paying the bill today, but we will not use up the insurance until later.
- Transaction 5 is related to transaction 2 so we classify it the same as item 2, accrued revenue.
- Transaction 6 is an accrued expense because we have already incurred an expense, but we will not pay it until later.
- Transaction 7 is related to transactions 2 and 5 so we classify it the same, accrued revenue.
- Transaction 8 is related to transaction 6 so we classify it the same, accrued expense.

SUMMARY

Chapter 6 introduced the accrual basis of accounting. This chapter expands upon that introduction by adding the concepts of accruals and deferrals. Accruals and deferrals are about timing differences. The accrual basis of accounting strives to record Revenue in the time period in which it is earned. If cash is received before Revenue is earned then we should put off, or defer, recording Revenue until later. If Revenue is earned before we receive the cash from the customer, then we should go ahead and record, or accrue, the Revenue now.

The accrual basis of accounting also strives to record Expenses in the time period in which they are incurred to help us earn Revenue. If cash is paid before an Expense is incurred then we should put off, or defer, recording Expense until later. If Expense is incurred before we pay cash, then we should go ahead and record, or accrue, the Expense now.

The accrual basis of accounting attempts to give an entity recognition for the work they have done in the period they have done it; that is, we want to recognize Revenue in the period you did the work or earned it, even if the cash will be received later, or earlier. Likewise, it is only consistent that if you are going to record Revenues when you did the work then you should record Expenses whenever you incur them, even if you will pay for them later, or earlier.

Accruals and deferrals are the foundation of the accrual basis of accounting. They are some of the most important concepts covered in this course. Unfortunately, they are also one of the most difficult areas of Financial Accounting for many students. You may need to reread this chapter several times before you are ready to move onto Chapter 8.

CHAPTER 8

ADJUSTMENTS, PART I

INTRODUCTION

Chapters 6 and 7 discussed the accrual basis of accounting, introduced accruals and deferrals, and provided some illustrations of transaction analysis with accruals and deferrals. A subset of accruals and deferrals is referred to as adjustments, which are the subject of Chapters 8 and 9.

ADJUSTMENTS

The word adjust could mean to change or update. In the context of this class, it means to change or update certain items before preparing financial statements at the end of an accounting period. Simply due to the passage of time, some items on our records become stale or outdated and need updating before preparing financial statements.

Let's illustrate adjusting entries by continuing with the example from Chapter 6. Assume it is the end of the year, December 31, 20X1, and the company is preparing for "year end." This is just a catch phrase for the things we need to do before we can generate accurate financial statements at the end of the year, or any period (e.g., monthly, quarter) for that matter.

For the Chapter 6 example, here are a few sample adjustments. Please print out Table 8.1 and record your answers as we go through them.

Financial Accounting: A Course for All Majors, pp. 57–66

Adjustment 1 (A1): A physical count reveals that supplies on hand at year were $300.

The records currently show that we have $1,800 of supplies on hand, the amount purchased on May 1 in transaction 1. However, due to the passage of time some supplies have been used up and, perhaps for practical reasons, there was no adjustments made as they were used between May and December. For small items like office supplies this is not uncommon as it is often not practical to record something as used up minute-by-minute or day-by-day. Rather, we just update the item periodically as we are attempting to do now.

The records show we have $1,800 of office supplies on hand but, in fact, we have counted the office supplies on hand and only have $300. What adjustment needs to be made to our records to make the books agree with reality? The books show $1,800 of supplies, but the reality is we only have $300 of supplies on hand. The adjusting entry is what it takes to get from where we are currently at on our books ($1,800) to what actually exists ($300).

This adjustment would be classified as a deferred expense because we initially recorded the item as an Asset when we paid for it. Later, when we use up the Asset it becomes an Expense. Defer means to delay, or put off. What we are delaying in this case is the recognition of the Expense until such time as we have used up the related Asset, office supplies.

Adjustment 2 (A2): The company received some cash from customers on August 1st in transaction 3. It is now December 31st.

We received $24,000 from a customer on August 1st in advance payment for services to be performed evenly over the next 6 months. It is now December 31st. How much of this $24,000 have we now earned? First, figure out how much this would be per month and then count how many months have elapsed. When we received this money from customers on August 1st we recorded it as Unearned Revenue. The fact that we have now done some of the work means we can take an amount out of Unearned Revenue and put it into Revenue. We refer to this as "recognizing," or recording, Revenue.

This adjustment would be classified as a deferred revenue since we initially recorded the amount received as a Liability, Unearned Revenue, and then later recognized the Revenue. What we put off, or deferred, was the recognition of the Revenue until such time as we had provided the good or service and therefore earned it.

Table 8.1. Chapter 8 Transaction Analysis Workpaper

	ASSETS (A)					= LIABILITIES (L)		+ EQUITY (EQ)			
									Retained Earnings (RE)		
									Net Income (NI)		
Trans.	Cash Operating	Accounts Receivable	Office Supplies	Prepaid Insurance		Unearned Revenue	Accounts Payable	Contributed Capital	Revenues (R)	Expenses (EX)	Dividends (D)
1	($1,800)		$1,800								
2		$10,000							$10,000		
3	$24,000					$24,000					
4	($3,600)			$3,600							
5	$6,000	($6,000)									
6							$1,500			($1,500)	
7	$4,000	($4,000)									
8	($1,500)						($1,500)				
Subtotal	**$27,100**	**$0**	**$1,800**	**$3,600**		**$24,000**	**$0**		**$10,000**	**($1,500)**	
A1											
A2											
A3											
Subtotal											

Adjustment 3 (A3): The company paid their annual property insurance on September 1st in transaction 4. It is now December 31st.

How much of the insurance is now used up? First, figure out how much this would be per month and then count how many months have elapsed. When we paid for the insurance in advance we recorded the amount as an Asset, Prepaid Insurance. What happens to an Asset when it is used up and no longer has any future value? Yes, it becomes an Expense.

This adjustment would be classified as a deferred expense for the same reasons that adjustment 1 above would be classified as a deferred expense. The answers to this exercise appear in Table 8.2 so that you may check your work.

ADJUSTMENTS: A SUBSET OF ACCRUALS AND DEFERRALS

Adjustments are subsets of the broader concepts of accruals and deferrals. Adjustments are updates made to the financial records at the end of an accounting period to help make sure things are current and up-to-date before preparing financial statements. All adjustments are either accruals or deferrals.

However, adjustments are just a subset of accruals and deferrals so not all accruals and deferrals are adjustments. Accruals and deferrals could happen at any time throughout the year. Accruals and deferrals become adjustments when they occur near the end of a financial period. Next we will discuss a common adjustment for each of the two types of accruals and each of the two types of deferrals.

ACCRUAL ADJUSTMENTS

Accrued Revenue. A common adjustment is when a business ships something to a customer just before the end of the year. The goal of the Accrued Revenue adjusting entry is to make sure we recognize Revenue for all the transactions we have earned by year end. If we shipped the product to the customer in, say, 20X1, then we should record the revenue in 20X1. This would mean recording an increase to Accounts Receivable and an increase to Revenue in 20X1. This is easier said than done when goods or services are provided to customers near year end. Without some conscious effort, these transactions might easily get recorded in 20X2 (which is incorrect since we actually provided the good or service in 20X1).

Table 8.2. Chapter 8 Completed Transaction Analysis Workpaper

	ASSETS (A)				= LIABILITIES (L)		+ EQUITY (EQ)			
								Retained Earnings (RE)		
	Cash	Accounts	Office	Prepaid	Unearned	Accounts	Contributed	Net Income (NI)		
Trans.	Operating	Receivable	Supplies	Insurance	Revenue	Payable	Capital	Revenues (R)	Expenses (EX)	Dividends (D)
1	($1,800)		$1,800							
2		$10,000						$10,000		
3	$24,000				$24,000					
4	($3,600)			$3,600						
5	$6,000	($6,000)								
6						$1,500			($1,500)	
7	$4,000	($4,000)								
8	($1,500)					($1,500)				
Subtotal	**$27,100**	**$0**	**$1,800**	**$3,600**	**$24,000**	**$0**		**$10,000**	**($1,500)**	
A1			($1,500)						($1,500)	
A2					($20,000)			$20,000		
A3				($1,200)					($1,200)	
Subtotal	$27,100	$0	$300	$2,400	$4,000	$0		$30,000	($4,200)	

Accrued Expense. Another common adjustment is to make sure that all the costs associated with, say, 20X1 are recorded in 20X1. There are usually costs such as utilities and wages that have been incurred but potentially not recorded. The goal of the Accrued Expense adjusting entry is to make sure all the costs of a time period are recorded in that time period. Therefore, we would need to record Accrued Expense as a year-end adjustment by increasing Accounts Payable and reducing Equity (Expense). Again, without a bit of thought it would be quite easy for some costs that were incurred near the end of an accounting period to not get recorded until the next period.

Remember, a critical point of accruals, deferrals, and adjustments is to make sure that Revenues are recorded in the period they are earned and Expenses are recorded in the period they are incurred to help the entity generate Revenues.

For both Accrued Revenue and Accrued Expense the adjusting entry is to record the *initial transaction* before the cash is received or paid. When accruals first occur, by definition no cash is received or paid. And, when no cash is received or paid it is much easier to lose track of the transaction and not get it recorded on our records.

DEFERRAL ADJUSTMENTS

Deferrals are a bit different. By definition with a deferral we are receiving or paying cash first, then earning Revenue or incurring an Expense later. Typically, the receipt or payment of cash gets recorded during the year, but an adjusting entry is required to update the transaction due to the passage of time. With deferrals, the adjusting entry is to record the *subsequent transaction* of earning Revenue or incurring the Expense.

Deferred Revenue. Consider a retailer that sells gift cards during the year. The initial sale of gift cards probably gets recorded as they occur because this transaction involves cash. Cash is updated frequently in our records and cash is constantly being monitored by an independent third party, our bank. So, the initial sales transactions are not the focus of the adjusting entry. The concern at year end is whether the account balance for Unearned Revenue is accurate. What portion of Unearned Revenue has been earned by year end and should therefore be counted as Revenue? Once we answer this question we make an adjustment to reduce the Liability, Unearned Revenue, and increase the Equity account, Revenue (see Example 1).

Deferred Expense. By definition, the initial transaction involved with a Deferred, or Prepaid, Expense is to pay cash for something. That something has not been used up, consumed, or expired yet so we record an Asset, like Prepaid Insurance. The question at year-end, and the focus of

Example 1. On November 1, 20X1, assume you received an advance payment of $750 from a customer in exchange for services to be provided evenly over the next 5 months. The answers appear at the end of this chapter.

(a) How much is Revenue for 20X1? That is, how much of the total have you earned by December 31, 20X1?
(b) How much is Revenue for 2008? That is, how much of the total will you earn in the next year, 20X2?
(c) What balance should exist in the Unearned Revenue account on December 31, 20X1? Unearned Revenue is a Liability account and it should represent the obligation that an entity has to provide future goods or services as of a particular date. In this case, what is the amount of the firm's obligation to provide future services as of December 31, 20X1?
(d) What would be the amount of the adjusting entry on December 31, 20X1? The amount of the adjusting entry would be whatever adjustment is needed to get the account from where it is (before the adjustment) to its correct balance (after the adjustment) on December 31, 20X1.

the adjustment, is whether the account balance for Prepaid Insurance is accurate. For example, do we still have this much Prepaid Insurance, or has some of it expired merely due to the passage of time? If some of it has expired, then we need to record an adjustment to reduce the Asset, Prepaid Insurance, and reduce Equity (Expense).

Example 2. Assume you prepaid insurance for $3,000 for one year on September 1, 20X1. The answers appear at the end of this chapter.

(a) How much is an Expense for 20X1? To answer this question, think about what portion is used up during 20X1.
(b) How much is an expense for 20X2? To answer this question, think about what portion is used up during 20X2.
(c) What balance should exist in the Prepaid Insurance account on December 31, 20X1? Prepaid Insurance is an Asset so to answer this question you need to think about what portion of the total has not yet been used by December 31, 20X1. An Asset is something that will provide future benefit so only the portion that is not used up by year end should remain in Prepaid Insurance on December 31, 20X1.

Example 2 continues on next page.

Example 2 continued from previous page.

(d) What would be the amount of the adjusting entry on December 31, 20X1? The amount of the adjusting entry would be whatever adjustment is needed to get the account from where it is (before the adjustment) to its correct balance (after the adjustment) on December 31, 20X1.

SUMMARY

Adjustments are updates made to the financial records at or near the end of a time period to help ensure the financial statements are complete and accurate.

For adjustments that can be classified as accruals, they involve recording the initial transaction associated with the event. The initial transaction means the event giving rise to the accrual, such as the shipment of goods to a customer or the incurrence of a cost like utilities or payroll.

For adjustments that can be classified as deferrals, they involve recording the subsequent event associated with the transaction. The subsequent event means that which follows after the initiating event. For example, in the gift card example, the initiating event is the retailer selling the gift card to a customer; the subsequent event is the retailer honoring the gift card when it is later presented to the retailer as payment for goods or services.

Adjustments can be rather simple on the one hand, but deceptively difficult on the other hand. Some people find them to be intuitively obvious, while others struggle greatly with the concept. If it were easy for everyone, we would transition to another topic. However, our experience suggests otherwise, so Chapter 9 will continue with the topic of adjustments.

SOLUTIONS TO CHAPTER EXAMPLES

Example 1. On November 1, 20X1, assume you received an advance payment of $750 from a customer in exchange for services to be provided evenly over the next 5 months.

(a) How much is revenue for 20X1? This is a payment for 5 months and 2 of those 5 months will be in 20X1 so the answer would be $750 * (2 / 5) = $300.

(b) How much is revenue for 20X2? I'd take the easy way out here and start with the total and subtract my answer to (a) above, or $750 – $300 = $450. Another approach is to recognize that this is a payment for 5 months and 3 of those 5 months will be in 20X2 so the answer would be $750 * (3 / 5) = $450.

(c) What balance should exist in the Unearned Revenue account on December 31, 20X1? The balance would be the amount not yet earned as of that date so it should be the same as the answer to (b) above, $450. That is, the amount that will be used up in 20X2 is the same as the amount that is not yet used up as of December 31, 20X1.

(d) What would be the amount of the adjusting entry on December 31, 20X1? When we received the payment on November 1, 20X1, we increased Cash and increased Unearned Revenue for the total of $750. On December 31, 20X1, the Unearned Revenue account will still have this account balance of $750. However, by December 31, 20X1, we will have earned $300 of that total, so we need to reduce Unearned Revenue by $300 and increase Revenue for the same amount. It is very important to note here that after this adjustment the Unearned Revenue will have an account balance of ($750 – $300) $450, which is consistent with the answer in (c) above.

Example 2. Assume you prepaid insurance for $3,000 for 1 year on September 1, 20X1.

(a) How much of the $3,000 total is an Expense for 20X1? Another way of saying this is, how much of the total is used up during 20X1? Since this is a 12-month policy and 4 months (September, October, November, and December) will occur in 20X1, then we'd argue that 4 / 12, or one-third, is used up in 20X1 and is therefore an Expense. The answer is $3,000 * (4 / 12) = $1,000.

(b) How much of the $3,000 total is an Expense for 20X2? Once you've answered (a) correctly the easiest way to do this is start with the total and subtract the answer to (a), or $3,000 – $1,000 = $2,000. We are taking a total cost of $3,000 and deciding what portion of that total should be allocated to 20X1 and 20X2. There's a check figure of sorts here in that the amount you allocate to 20X1 plus the amount you allocate to 20X2 must equal the total of $3,000. Another way to answer this question is to recognize that 8 months of the policy period (January through August) will occur in 20X2 so the answer would be $3,000 * (8 / 12) = $2,000.

(c) What balance should exist in the Prepaid Insurance account on December 31, 20X1? The balance that should exist in the Asset account, Prepaid Insurance, on any date is the amount that is not yet used. On December 31, 20X1, the amount not yet used up would be the same as the answer to (b) above, $2,000.

(d) What would be the amount of the adjusting entry on December 31, 20X1? When we paid for the policy on September 1, 20X1, we decreased Cash and increased Prepaid Insurance for $3,000. So, on December 31, 20X1, the Prepaid Insurance account would still have $3,000 in it. If you think about your answers to (a) and (c) above, we hope you'll agree that we need to adjust this account balance to account for the fact that one-third of the insurance is now expired, or used up. The adjusting entry would be to reduce the Prepaid Insurance account by $1,000 and record Insurance Expense for the same amount, $1,000. Note that after this adjustment the Prepaid Insurance account will have a balance of ($3,000 – $1,000) $2,000, which is consistent with the answer to (c) above.

CHAPTER 9

ADJUSTMENTS, PART II

INTRODUCTION

One of the more difficult topics in Financial Accounting is often adjustments. The purpose of this chapter is to provide another perspective on adjustments. Our focus in this chapter will be on those adjustments classified as deferrals because we have found these to be the most problematic for the typical student.

THE "A" WORDS: ALLOCATION AND ADJUSTMENT

The basic concept associated with deferrals is allocation; we are allocating a large amount between two or more periods. In fact, the other "A" word, allocation, is used a lot when talking about adjustments.

Here is a conceptual example. A business pays its annual insurance policy on October 1, 20X1. The policy covers the period October 1, 20X1, through September 30, 20X2. For accounting purposes the company prepares financial statements on a calendar year basis from January through December of each year. What portion of the payment made on October 1, 20X1, is an expense for the year 20X1? 20X2?

Financial Accounting: A Course for All Majors, pp. 67–72

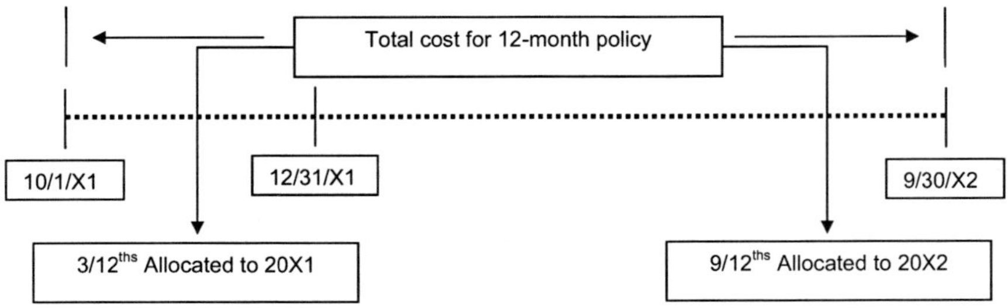

Figure 9.1. Allocation of prepaid insurance between two periods.

Let's look at Figure 9.1 to see how we should allocate this cost between the two calendar years, 20X1 and 20X2. Since the total cost for the 12-month policy covers two accounting periods, 20X1 and 20X2, we allocate this cost between the two periods. Initially, when we pay for the policy on October 1, 20X1, we record a decrease in Operating Cash Flow and an increase in Prepaid Insurance.

On December 31, 20X1, we make an adjusting entry to show that 3/12ths of the total is now used up and is an Expense for the period 20X1. As of December 21, 20X1, the remaining 9/12ths is still an Asset, Prepaid Insurance, because it has not yet been used up. It will be used up and become an Expense in 20X2. Finally, on September 30, 20X2, we would need to show that the remaining 9/12ths has now been used up and is an Expense for the period 20X2.

TRANSACTION ANALYSIS EXAMPLE

Let's assume the total cost of insurance for the 12-month period is $3,000. Figure 9.2 is an illustration to go along with this example:

In workpaper format the initial cost would be recorded with a decrease to Operating Cash Flow and an increase to Prepaid Insurance as follows in Table 9.1:

Table 9.1. Cash Payment for Prepaid Insurance

Date	*Cash-Operating*	*Prepaid Insurance*	*Insurance Expense*
10/1/X1	– 3,000	+ 3,000	

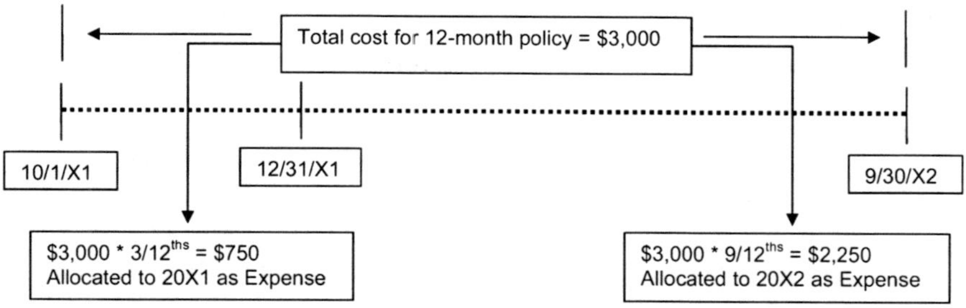

Figure 9.2. Numerical example of allocating prepaid insurance between two periods.

On December 31, 20X1, an adjusting entry would be made to show that a portion, 3/12ths, of the total has been used up and is an expense for the period 20X1, as shown in Table 9.2:

Table 9.2. Adjusting Entry to Record the Portion of Prepaid Insurance Used Up

Date	*Cash-Operating*	*Prepaid Insurance*	*Insurance Expense*
10/1/X1	– 3,000	+ 3,000	
12/31/X1 Adjustment		– 750	– 750

This adjustment allocates 3/12ths of the total cost to the accounting period 20X1 where it will be recorded as Insurance Expense on the 20X1 Income Statement. What's left in each column after making this adjustment?

Table 9.3. Account Balances After Adjustment to Record Insurance Expense

Date	*Cash-Operating*	*Prepaid Insurance*	*Insurance Expense*
10/1/X1	– 3,000	+ 3,000	
12/31/X1 Adjustment		– 750	– 750
12/31/X1 Adjustment Balances	**– 3,000**	**+ 2,250**	**– 750**

The account balances on 12/31/X1 show that we spent $3,000 cash on insurance during 20X1, that we still had $2,250 of Prepaid Insurance at year end, and that $750 of insurance was used up during 20X1. This is shown in Table 9.3.

Please note a critical point for answering test questions related to this topic. Even if you understand everything in this chapter, you will still miss exam questions if you do not comprehend the following point. Some questions will ask you for the amount of the adjusting entry on, say, 12/31/X1. In Table 9.3, the answer is $750. Other questions will ask you for the account balance in Prepaid Insurance on 12/31/X1. That is, the portion not used up yet as of year end. The answer in Table 9.3 is $2,250. Read each question very carefully to determine whether you are being asked for the amount of the adjusting entry, which will be the portion used up, or the balance in Prepaid Insurance, which will be the remaining portion not yet used up.

Finally, on 9/30/X2 we will need to show that the remaining portion of the Prepaid Insurance is now used up, leaving a balance of zero in Prepaid Insurance, as shown in Table 9.4.

Table 9.4. Adjustment in Year X2 to Record Insurance Expense

Date	*Cash-Operating*	*Prepaid Insurance*	*Insurance Expense*
10/1/X1	– 3,000	+ 3,000	
12/31/X1 Adjustment		– 750	– 750
12/31/X1 Adjustment Balances	**– 3,000**	**+ 2,250**	**– 750**
9/30/X2 Adjustment		– 2,250	– 2,250

A REVIEW OF SOME KEY OPERATING-TYPE TRANSACTIONS

The material in this course is inherently cumulative. It is difficult to do well in subsequent chapters if you failed to comprehend the material in earlier chapters. Since this is a relatively short chapter, we are going to take this opportunity to present a review of some key operating-type transactions in Table 9.5. This review includes transactions for cash revenues, cash expenses, accrued revenues, accrued expenses, deferred revenues, and deferred expenses. It is presented in a concise, transaction analysis format and we hope it will be useful as a quick reference guide for some of the key concepts covered so far in this book.

SUMMARY

This is a relatively brief, follow-up chapter on adjusting entries. Some people find it quite helpful to draw a diagram like the one used in this

Table 9.5. Transaction Analysis Review for Operating-Type Activities Including Accruals and Deferrals

	ASSETS			=	LIABILITIES		+	EQUITY	
	Operating Cash	Accounts Receivable	Prepaid Asset		Accounts Payable	Unearned Revenue		Revenue	Expense
1. Business receives cash in exchange for providing services (Cash Revenue).	+							+	
2. Business pays cash in exchange for a day-to-day operating cost (Cash Expense).	-								-
3. Business earns revenue in exchange for a customer's promise to pay (Accrued Revenue - Initial).		+						+	
4. Business collects cash from the customer in the preceding transaction (Accrued Revenue-Subsequent).	+	-							
5. Business incurs a day-to-day operating cost but has not paid the bill yet (Accrued Expense - Initial).					+				-
6. Business pays cash for the bill in the preceding transaction (Accrued Expense - Subsequent).	-				-				
7. Business receives cash from a customer for services to be provided in the future (Deferred Revenue - Initial).	+					+			
8. Business provides the services for the customer in the preceding transaction (Deferred Revenue-Subsequent).						-		+	
9. Business pays cash for something that will be used up in day-to-day operations in the future (Deferred Expense-Initial).	-		+						
10. Business uses up the item acquired in the preceding transaction (Deferred Expense - Subsequent).			-						-

chapter so that they can visualize the allocation process. Others do quite well without a diagram so it is a matter of what works best to help you understand this material. For those of you continuing to struggle with adjusting entries, we hope this alternative explanation is helpful.

CHAPTER 10

THE ACCOUNTING CYCLE

INTRODUCTION

Chapters 6-9 were about the accrual basis of accounting. Closely related to accrual basis accounting are the notions of accruals and deferrals, which are transactions with timing differences between when cash is received or paid and when revenue or expense is earned or incurred. Adjustments, or adjusting entries, are made at the end of an accounting period to help ensure that all revenues earned during the period have been properly recorded, and all expenses that have been incurred have been recognized.

Chapter 2 introduced Financial Accounting as a "black box" process that converts inputs (economic transactions) into outputs (three, major financial statements). This chapter will give you a glimpse into this black box without burdening you too much with technical details. Our philosophy in this chapter is to acquaint you with the process and vocabulary so that you could interact with people in accounting and finance actually doing the detailed record keeping.

Financial Accounting: A Course for All Majors, pp. 73–78

THE ACCOUNTING CYCLE

The Accounting Cycle is the phrase used to describe the recurring process that takes place each accounting period as an entity processes inputs (economic transactions) into outputs (three, major financial statements). Before we list the major steps in The Accounting Cycle we should note that many of the terms in this chapter are relics of the past when record keeping was done manually with pencil and paper.

This chapter will cover five, major steps in The Accounting Cycle:

1. Journalization in the General Journal
2. Posting from the General Journal to the General Ledger
3. Adjustments, or Adjusting Entries
4. Preparing Three, Major Financial Statements
5. Closing All Temporary Accounts

The five steps above occur in sequence and you should go ahead and memorize the five steps in the correct order now. The remainder of this chapter will explain the five steps in the sequence presented above.

1. Journalization in the General Journal

Back in the old days of pencil and paper record keeping, economic transactions were recorded in roughly chronological order as they occurred. The book they were recorded in was called the *General Journal* and the process of initially recording transactions in the General Journal was called *Journalizing* or *Journalization*. Even though most entities have transitioned to electronic record keeping, these terms are still in use today. The General Journal is now commonly an electronic file in a computer system, but the terminology from the old days is still in use.

To recap, step 1 is simply to capture, or record, the effect of each economic transaction. This is done in the General Journal in roughly chronological order through a process referred to as Journalization.

2. Posting From the General Journal to the General Ledger

Transactions are initially recorded in the General Journal in chronological order. The next step is to update each account for the effects of a transaction so that we can have current account balances.

Let's say that a business makes a cash sale for $100 to a customer. In step 1 we would record this, or journalize it, in the General Journal as an increase to Cash and an increase to Revenue. The two accounts involved are Cash and Revenue. Now, visualize 10, or a 100, or a 1,000 other transactions being recorded in sequence as they occur. Step 1 is a critical first step to get the information initially entered into our record keeping system. However, step 1 by itself does not give us updated information about individual account balances, like Cash or Revenue.

The *General Ledger* can be thought of as a book with each page in the book representing a specific account, like Cash or Revenue. In step 2, the information from the General Journal is *transferred, or posted,* to the appropriate page in the General Ledger. For our cash sale above, this means that we would transfer the increase in Cash from the General Journal entry to the page for Cash in the General Ledger. We would also transfer the increase to Revenue from the entry in the General Journal to the page for Revenue in the General Ledger. We illustrate this in Figure 10.1.

To recap, posting is simply transferring information from one file, or place, to another. In step 2, information is transferred from each entry in the General Journal to the appropriate page(s), or account(s), in the General Ledger. The General Ledger, then, provides us with a page for each

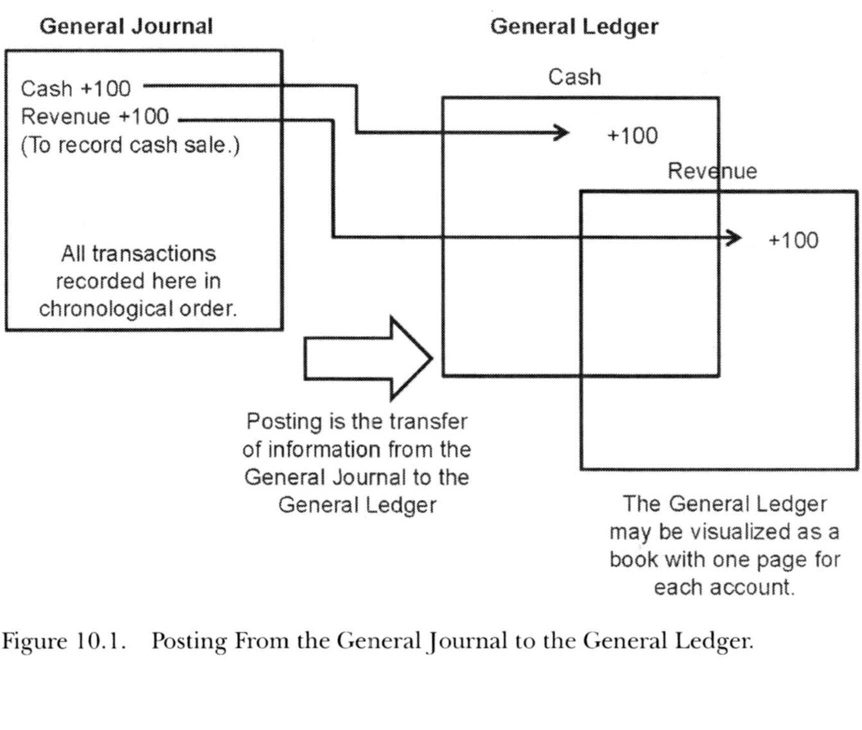

Figure 10.1. Posting From the General Journal to the General Ledger.

account so that if we want to know, say, how much our current balance is for Cash we can go to the Cash page in the General Ledger to find the answer. We can do the same thing for any other account, provided all transactions were properly journalized in step 1, and properly posted in step 2.

Before we proceed to step 3, just think about steps 1 and 2 taking place repeatedly for each and every economic transaction throughout an accounting period.

3. Adjustments, or Adjusting Entries

Chapters 8 and 9 discussed adjusting entries so there is not too much more to say about them here. We simply want to discuss them in the context of their place in the accounting cycle.

In step 3, we are now at the end of an accounting period. Before preparing financial statements we step back and ask ourselves whether all of our account balances are up-to-date. Have we earned any Revenue that has not been recorded? In the process of earning Revenue, have we incurred any Expenses that are not yet recorded?

The other thing we should note in step 3 is that the end of the accounting period is a busy time for accounting and financing staff. They are trying to make sure everything in the system is accurate and complete before preparing financial statements. In some cases, things that should have gotten done earlier did not and now it is time to catch up.

The best analogy we can give you is getting your personal records together so that you can prepare your annual income tax return, or have it prepared for you. In a perfect world, we would document transactions as they occur and maintain accurate records so that the completion of the annual tax return would be routine. However, we don't live in a perfect world, people are busy and they don't like to keep records, and so we often end up with a bit of chaos leading up to the deadline for our income tax returns. A similar phenomenon occurs at year end in the accounting cycle.

4. Preparing Three, Major Financial Statements

Step 1 has recorded the effects of each and every economic transaction in the General Journal, step 2 has posted this information from the General Journal to the General Ledger, and step 3 has examined each account to make sure it is accurate and complete.

In step 4 we are ready to generate the output of the financial accounting process. The Balance Sheet, Income Statement, and Statement of Cash Flows, are the three reports that tell the economic story of an entity.

We haven't looked at any real world financial statements yet, but when we do you will see that they can be quite condensed. For example, Wal-Mart's financial statements are no more than one page each. The Balance Sheet is one page, the Income Statement is one page, and the Statement of Cash Flows is one page. Can you imagine how many transactions occur in a year for Wal-Mart, all to be summarized in about three pages? The point is that financial statements are the reports we use to summarize activity. People have time to read and analyze three pages, but they do not have time to study millions of individual transactions.

5. Closing All Temporary Accounts

The final step in The Accounting Cycle is to close all Temporary Accounts. This will be entirely new to us in this chapter so we need to be careful to explain terminology.

First, *"to close" or "closing" means to bring an account balance to zero.*

Second, *Temporary Accounts are those that contain activity for only one accounting period.* In contrast, Permanent Accounts maintain an ongoing record of activities for, literally, the entire lifetime of an entity.

Third, the Temporary Accounts are *all Revenue accounts, all Expense accounts,* and *the Dividend account.* As a reminder, these are all Equity accounts; that is, they appeared under Equity in our transaction workpaper.

Fourth, the Permanent Accounts include *all Assets,* or those that we would not want to be zeroed out at year end. Permanent Accounts also include *all Liabilities,* or those that we probably wish would disappear at year end, but they do not! Permanent Accounts include *some Equity accounts, namely Contributed Capital and Retained Earnings.*

With these terms and definitions behind us, we can now state fairly concisely what takes place in the "closing process": *the amounts in all the Temporary Accounts are moved to a Permanent Account, Retained Earnings.*

After "closing" all Revenue accounts, all Expense accounts, and the Dividend account will have a zero balance; it is not that the amounts in those accounts disappeared, but rather they were moved to a permanent location, the Retained Earnings account. As we begin a new accounting period, the Revenue, Expense, and Dividend accounts will now accumulate information for the current period only. Maintaining Temporary Equity accounts allows us to isolate the activity that took place in the current accounting period only without having to sort through transactions and activity that may have taken place years ago.

This would probably be a good time to elaborate on Retained Earnings, which is a Permanent Equity account. *Retained Earnings contains the undistributed, lifetime net income of an entity.* Undistributed means kept within the entity to finance future operations or growth, lifetime means since the beginning of the entity, and net income is the entity's excess of Revenues over Expenses.

Retained Earnings is not like Cash. Some people look at The Balance Sheet, see Retained Earnings, and start thinking of ways to spend it. Retained Earnings is not Cash that can be spent. It is the undistributed, lifetime net income of an entity. It represents all the money the company has made but not returned to its owners in the form of a dividend. That does not mean it has all of this money in the bank in a checking account.

For example, at a personal level if you maintained a Retained Earnings account it would show your lifetime earnings (actually, the Social Security office sort of does this for you, but that's another story). Stop and think about what your total, lifetime earnings have been. Now, compare this to what you have in your checking account. The point is that your lifetime earnings represent what you have earned over time, but you may have used those earnings to buy other assets or to pay off liabilities. The same is true with a company. Retained Earnings is the undistributed, lifetime net income of an entity, but it is not a stockpile of cash that is available for spending. If you want to know how much cash an entity has, look at the cash account, not the Retained Earnings account.

SUMMARY

The Accounting Cycle is the series of steps that an entity goes through each accounting period (usually a year, but it could be for shorter intervals like a month or quarter) in order to go from inputs (economic transactions) to outputs (financial statements). Although the series of steps is well known and routine, the actual process can be chaotic as we attempt to collect, measure, record, and summarize what could be millions of transactions and report them in three, concise, financial statements.

CHAPTER 11

THE CLASSIFIED BALANCE SHEET

INTRODUCTION

Chapters 1–10 have taken us through an introduction to Financial Accounting, transaction analysis, the accrual basis of accounting, and the accounting cycle. Our focus in the next two chapters will shift a bit to an overview of The Balance Sheet in this chapter and The Income Statement in Chapter 12.

THE CLASSIFIED BALANCE SHEET

The term classified above just means a balance sheet with certain, commonly used, categories of Assets, Liabilities, and Equity. The outline for a typical, classified balance sheet follows:

Financial Accounting: A Course for All Majors, pp. 79–83

ASSETS

Current Assets (Liquidity Order)

- **Cash**
- **Accounts Receivable**
- **Inventory**
- **Prepaid Assets/Supplies**

Investments

Property, Plant, and Equipment/Tangible Assets

Intangible Assets

LIABILITIES

Current Liabilities

- **Accounts Payable**
- **Notes Payable**
- **Unearned Revenue**

Long-Term, or Noncurrent, Liabilities

Notes Payable

Bonds Payable

Pension Liabilities

EQUITY

Contributed Capital

Retained Earnings

ASSETS

Current Assets. In the context of a classified balance sheet, current means something that will happen within one year from the balance sheet date. Anything that will occur more than 1 year from the balance sheet date is referred to as noncurrent, or long-term.

Current assets include Cash, items that will normally be converted into Cash within 1 year (i.e., Accounts Receivable and Inventory), and items that will normally be consumed or used up within 1 year (i.e., Prepaid Assets or Supplies). Current Assets are listed in order of their liquidity, or nearness to Cash.

Cash is as close to Cash as you can get so it is listed first. Accounts Receivable are only one step away from Cash (the collection step) so they are listed next. Inventory is viewed as being two steps away from Cash. First, the business will need to sell the inventory to customers, potentially on account. Second, the business will need to collect the resulting Account Receivable. Finally, items that are consumed or used up typically do not get converted back to Cash at all so they are listed last in this section.

The remaining categories of assets are typically long-term, or noncurrent, assets. This means they will typically be held, owned, used, or controlled for more than one year from the balance sheet date.

Investments could be one of two types—owning or loaning. First, it is not uncommon for one company to buy ownership, or stock, in another company. For example, Microsoft might spot a small, but upcoming computer company and decide to buy stock in that company. This would be an Investment on Microsoft's balance sheet. Second, one company can lend money to another company. The company lending the money will record a Receivable in exchange for lending the other company money and they will classify this Receivable as an Investment on their balance sheet.

Property, Plant, and Equipment (PP&E) represents all the tangible assets that a business uses in its day-to-day business to help it earn revenues. Tangible here means something with physical substance like a desk, chair, car, computer, machinery, equipment, land, buildings, and so forth.

Intangible Assets are things with economic value but they lack the traditional notion of physical substance that sometimes is associated with assets. What has economic value but no physical substance? Common examples for businesses are Patents, Copyrights, and Licenses. These things all convey special economic privileges to the owner of the item and, therefore, have economic value. However, the only physical substance they possess is the paper that documents their existence.

LIABILITIES

Current Liabilities. Current has the same meaning with liabilities as it did with assets; current liabilities are those that will come due and require payment, or otherwise be extinguished, within 1 year from the balance sheet date. Long-term, or noncurrent, liabilities are those that will become due beyond 1 year from the balance sheet date.

Common current liabilities are Accounts Payable, which arise from our day-to-day operations when a vendor, or supplier, allows us to charge items. Notes Payable arises from borrowing transactions when we borrow money from, say, a local bank to help finance our business. Unearned Revenue is that liability that arises when we are paid in advance for something that we have not yet provided.

Noncurrent, or long-term, liabilities include Notes Payable. We put Notes Payable in both Current and Noncurrent Liabilities to make a point. Notes Payable would be current if the debt were due within 1 year from the balance sheet date; Notes Payable would be noncurrent if it were due more than 1 year from the balance sheet date. The 1 year cutoff is just an arbitrary dividing line we use to distinguish between the near term and the more distant future.

Noncurrent liabilities also include something called Bonds Payable. A bond is just a fancy name for an IOU. When a company or government borrows money they often give the lender an IOU, or bond, in return. This bond simply describes the repayment terms and conditions and provides the lender with documentation of the lending transaction.

Noncurrent liabilities could include other things, but I've only listed one more, Pension Liabilities. This has become a big issue recently with the U.S. auto industry. For decades our U.S. auto manufacturers promised health and retirement benefits to their employees. A promise today of a payment to be made in the future is a liability, and the auto manufacturers have accumulated some very large obligations to their retired workers. For example, it has been reported that more than $1,500 for every vehicle sold by General Motors goes to pay for so-called "legacy costs" or pension obligations. These costs are part of the reason why both Chrysler and General Motors entered bankruptcy during 2009.

EQUITY

There's really nothing new to report in this section. Contributed Capital, or Paid-in Capital, is the money that owners have put directly into the business in exchange for stock, or ownership interest. Retained Earnings is the undistributed, lifetime net income of the business.

Of the three sections on the balance sheet, Equity is sometimes the most difficult to comprehend. Perhaps that is because it does not have the physical substance of most Assets, nor the intuitive understanding that most of us have of Liabilities. Keep in mind that another way to think about Equity is Assets minus Liabilities equals Equity. That is, Equity is the difference between Assets and Liabilities.

SUMMARY

A classified balance sheet is just a balance sheet with some commonly used categories, or classifications. An important distinction on a classified balance sheet is current versus noncurrent. The arbitrary dividing line between the two is one year from the balance sheet date. Chapter 12 will continue with some details about the income statement.

CHAPTER 12

THE MULTIPLE-STEP INCOME STATEMENT

INTRODUCTION

Chapter 11 discussed The Classified Balance Sheet. This chapter will cover a brief introduction to merchandising transactions, followed by an overview of the Classified, or Multiple-Step, Income Statement.

THREE TYPES OF BUSINESSES

As a preliminary item before we get to the income statement, we need to mention three common types of businesses:

- *Service* businesses provide a, well, service to a customer. Examples of this category include a lawyer, doctor, or accountant.
- *Merchandising* businesses buy products from their suppliers, mark up the price, and resell them to their customers. Examples of this category include places like Wal-Mart, Target, and Claire's.
- *Manufacturing* businesses buy raw materials and employ people to build products. Examples include auto manufacturers like General Motors, Ford, and Chrysler.

Financial Accounting: A Course for All Majors, pp. 85–91

These are pure forms for the classroom and actual businesses sometimes blur the distinctions. For example, an auto mechanic is mostly a service business but as part of the service buys parts, marks up the price a bit, and includes them on our bill so it is a bit of a merchandising business.

Before we can introduce the Classified, or Multiple-Step, Income Statement we need to elaborate a bit on merchandising transactions. We will not discuss manufacturing businesses much further in this class. If you are required to take the second course in accounting, Managerial Accounting, manufacturing businesses are covered in some depth in that course.

A BRIEF INTRODUCTION TO MERCHANDISING TRANSACTIONS

A merchandising business buys product, which we'll call *Inventory,* or *Merchandise Inventory,* marks up the price, and makes it available for its customers to purchase. Let's go through the transactions of buying and selling inventory for a merchandising business.

First, assume a merchandising company buys inventory costing $60 for cash. This is shown in Table 12.1:

Table 12.1. Purchase of Inventory With Cash

	Operating Cash Flow	*Merchandise Inventory*	*Revenue / Sales*	*Expense / Cost of Goods Sold*
Purchase	– 60	+ 60		

This transaction would decrease Operating Cash Flow and Increase Merchandise Inventory. Merchandise Inventory represents the cost of items purchased with the intent of ultimately reselling them to customers.

Next, assume the business prices the item for sale at, say, $100 and a customer buys it. This is illustrated in Table 12.2:

Table 12.2. Sales of Inventory for Cash

	Operating Cash Flow	*Merchandise Inventory*	*Revenue / Sales*	*Expense / Cost of Goods Sold*
Purchase	– 60	+ 60		
Sale—Part 1	+ 100		+ 100	
Sale—Part 2		– 60		– 60
Subtotals	**+ 40**	**0**	**+ 100**	**– 60**

In Sale—Part 1 we have recorded the sale of the inventory to the customer for $100 cash. This transaction increases Revenue, which is also called *Sales* for a merchandising company, and increases Operating Cash Flow.

In Sale—Part 2 we have recorded the cost of what we sold as an Expense. That is, the company did not "make" $100 on the sale to the customer. The business received $100 cash from the customer, but the item sold cost the business $60 so we need to record that cost as an Expense. We will call the Expense associated with inventory sold to customers, *Cost of Goods Sold.*

If we look at the combined effects of the three entries now, or the subtotals line, we see the business brought in $40 of Operating Cash Flow from these transactions. The Merchandise Inventory account was first increased by $60, but later decreased by the same amount because we sold the item. What happens to an asset when it's gone or is used up? It becomes an Expense and the same is true with Merchandise Inventory. When we recorded the reduction in inventory we showed that the cost of the inventory had become an Expense called Cost of Goods Sold. The subtotals line shows Sales of $100, which reflects the total amount received for the item from the customer and Cost of Goods Sold for $60, which represents what that inventory cost the merchandising business.

Here is a new definition: *Sales minus Cost of Goods Sold equals Gross Profit.* In our example above, the merchandising business made a gross profit of $40 on the transactions. For now, just note that this is not the same as net income, or "profit". The merchandising business still has many other Expenses, like payroll and utilities. Gross Profit is just the difference between what they sold the item for versus what they paid for it.

THE CLASSIFIED, OR MULTIPLE-STEP, INCOME STATEMENT

Now, we can get to the focus of this chapter. In its simplest form, the Income Statement consists of:

	Revenues
Minus	Expenses
Equals	Net Income

This is referred to as a single-step income statement because no matter whether there are two Revenue accounts or 200, all of the Revenue is listed first. Then, no matter how many Expense accounts there might be they are all listed next and subtracted from the Revenues.

The Classified, or Multiple-Step, Income Statement just arranges Revenues and Expenses into categories:

	Sales (primary Revenue account for a merchandising firm)
Minus	Cost of Goods Sold (an Expense)
Equals	Gross Profit
Minus	Selling, General, and Administrative Expenses (SG&A)
Equals	Income from Operations, or Operating Income
Plus	Other Revenues or Gains
Minus	Other Expenses or Losses
Equals	Income before Income Taxes
Minus	Income Tax Expense
Equals	Net Income

The "bottom line," or Net Income, is exactly the same regardless of how the items above it are organized. The Multiple-Step Income Statement is just a common way to categorize, or classify, items on an income statement.

Figure 12.1 shows that the total Revenues in the single-step income statement have just been rearranged in the multiple-step income statement. The portion of Revenues that was derived from the company's primary day-to-day sales of goods and services to its customers is reported as Sales. The remaining portion of total Revenues that was incidental to the company's primary business is reported in the Other Revenues or Gains section of the multiple-step income statement.

Figure 12.2 shows that the total Expenses in the single-step income statement have also just been rearranged in the multiple-step income

Single-Step		Multiple-Step	
	Revenues →		Sales
Minus	Expenses	Minus	Cost of Goods Sold
		Equals	Gross Profit
		Minus	SG&A Expenses
		Equals	Operating Income
	(Revenues) →	Plus	Other Revenues or Gains
		Minus	Other Expenses or Losses
		Equals	Income before Income Taxes
		Minus	Income Tax Expense
Equals	Net Income	Equals	Net Income

Figure 12.1. Allocation of Revenues in the Multiple-Step Income Statement.

Single-Step		Multiple-Step	
	Revenues		Sales
Minus	Expenses	Minus	Cost of Goods Sold
		Equals	Gross Profit
		Minus	SG&A Expenses
		Equals	Operating Income
		Plus	Other Revenues or Gains
		Minus	Other Expenses or Losses
		Equals	Income before Income Taxes
		Minus	Income Tax Expense
Equals	Net Income	Equals	Net Income

Figure 12.2. Allocation of Expenses in the Multiple-Step Income Statement.

statement. The portion of total Expenses related to the cost of products purchased for, and subsequently resold to, customers is classified as Cost of Goods Sold. The additional costs the company incurred to provide goods and services to its customers are reported as SG&A Expense in the multiple-step income statement. The portion of total Expenses that was incidental to the company's primary business is reported in the Other Expenses and Losses section. Finally, the portion of total Expenses that represents corporate income taxes paid to governmental entities is reported as Income Tax Expense in the multiple-step income statement.

We hope it is clear from Figures 12.1 and 12.2 that the two formats are equivalent in content, but differ in format. How we choose to report an entity's Revenues and Expenses does not change the underlying total for either element. The rest of this chapter will elaborate on the individual components of the Multiple-Step Income Statement.

Sales is the primary Revenue account for a merchandising business. It represents the amounts received from customers in exchange for goods and services. Cost of Goods Sold is an Expense account that represents the cost of the items customers have purchased from the merchandising business.

Gross Profit was defined earlier as Sales minus Cost of Goods Sold. It represents the difference between what the merchandising business paid for an item versus what it received for that item from its customer.

Selling, General and Administrative Expenses (SG&A) include most of the other costs associated with running the day-to-day business. SG&A would include salaries, wages, and payroll costs associated with employees, utilities, and the costs associated with having a building, like property taxes and insurance.

Income from Operations, or Operating Income, is Gross Profit minus SG&A. It is a measure of how much money we made, before paying income taxes, from our day-to-day business operations.

Other Revenues or Gains are miscellaneous items that contribute to Revenue but are not the primary reason we are in business. For example, a retailer might have some revenue from interest earned on bank deposits, but interest revenue is not the primary way the retailer earns revenue.

The distinction between Revenue and Gains is subtle. Gains are one-time, nonrecurring items that just don't happen very much. Maybe a storm hits our business and our insurance is really good so we end up making money on the situation. Or, maybe we hit the equivalent of the lottery and have a one-time windfall. These items are highlighted and called Gains because someone reading the income statement needs to know that they probably will not happen again in the future. They are good events, yes, but not events that are likely to recur again anytime soon.

Other Expenses and Losses are the mirror image of Other Revenues and Gains. Other Expenses would include interest that we pay on borrowed money as well as other costs that really are not very closely associated with our day-to-day business. Losses are reductions in net income and Equity like Expenses, but they are one-time, nonrecurring items. An example of a Loss would be if a storm hit the business and we did not have any insurance.

Income before Income Taxes is all of the Revenues minus all of the Expenses, *except* Income Tax Expense. Most business entities must pay a corporate income tax on their income. Let's say the Income before Income Taxes was $100 and the corporate income tax rate was 40%. The Income Tax Expense would be ($100 * .40) $40, and the Net Income would be $100 minus $40, or $60.

Example: Assume a company's sales are $1,000, cost of goods sold $600, SG&A Expense $150, and the corporate tax rate is 40%. What are the company's gross profit, operating income, and net income? The answer appears at the end of the chapter.

SUMMARY

Financial statements in the United States are notorious for their differences, not uniformity. However, most balance sheets tend to follow the format described in Chapter 11 on the Classified Balance Sheet. Likewise, many (not all) published income statements tend to following the format described in this chapter and referred to as a Multiple-Step Income Statement.

Example Solution: Assume a company's sales are $1,000, cost of goods sold $600, SG&A Expense $150, and the corporate tax rate is 40%. What are the company's gross profit, operating income, and net income?: Figures in boldface are calculated from the information given.

Table 12.3. Solution to Multiple-Step Income Statement Problem

	Sales	$1,000
Minus	Cost of Goods Sold	600
Equals	Gross Profit	**400**
Minus	SG&A Expenses	150
Equals	Operating Income	**250**
Plus	Other Revenues or Gains	0
Minus	Other Expenses or Losses	0
Equals	Income before Income Taxes	**250**
Minus	Income Tax Expense 40%	**100**
Equals	Net Income	**$150**

CHAPTER 13

OPERATING ACTIVITIES

An Introduction to Bad Debts Expense

INTRODUCTION

As you will recall, the Statement of Cash Flows is organized into three categories: operating, investing, and financing cash flows. Our next step in this course will be to use this framework to discuss the activities of an organization. We will begin with five Chapters (13–17) on operating activities, one chapter (18) on investing activities, and then three Chapters (19–21) on financing activities.

A REVIEW OF BASIC REVENUE TRANSACTIONS

Let's begin with a refresher on some basic revenue transactions.

- Cash Transaction—A company provides a good or service to a customer and simultaneously receives payment: Operating Cash Flow increases and Revenue increases.
- Deferred Revenue—A company receives cash today in exchange for its promise to provide the customer a good or service in the future.

Financial Accounting: A Course for All Majors, pp. 93–100

Upon receipt of the cash, the company increases Operating Cash Flow and increases a liability, Unearned Revenue. Upon providing the good or service, and thereby earning the right to keep the money, they reduce Unearned Revenue and increase Revenue.

- Accrued Revenue—A company provides a good or service to a customer today in exchange for the customer's promise to pay in the future; this is commonly referred to as a "charge," or "credit" sale. The company is extending "credit" to its customer. Using the accrual basis of accounting we increase an asset, Accounts Receivable, and increase Revenue. When we later receive payment from the customer, we decrease Accounts Receivable and increase Operating Cash Flow.

Table 13.1 summarizes the effects of these three basic transactions:

Table 13.1. A Review of Basic Revenue Transactions

Transaction	*Before*	*Good / Services Provided*	*After*
Cash Sale	N/A	+ Op. Cash Flow + Revenue	N/A
Deferred Revenue	+ Op. Cash Flow + Unearned Revenue	– Unearned Revenue + Revenue	N/A
Accrued Revenue	N/A	+ Accounts Receivable + Revenue	– Accounts Receivable + Op. Cash Flow

Note in Table 13.1, *that Revenue is recognized at the same point in all three transactions—when the goods or services are provided to the customer.* The difference among the three types of transactions is when the company is paid for the good or service.

A PROBLEM WITH ACCRUED REVENUE: UNCOLLECTIBLE ACCOUNTS

With cash sales or with deferred revenue, the company has received payment for its goods or services. The same cannot be said for accrued revenues. This leads to a common question—what if the company does not get paid in the future (i.e., it cannot collect the related Account Receivable)?

First, we should clarify that when we initially record the accrued revenue we are assuming that we will collect payment from the customer. If we had compelling evidence to the contrary, wouldn't we demand payment in advance, or at the time of sale, or not sell to that customer in the first place?

Second, an easy way to avoid this problem is to not extend credit to our customers. Even though companies know they will experience this problem, many companies nevertheless do extend credit to their customers. This is based upon a logical evaluation of the benefits of extending credit to customers (i.e., credit is appealing to customers hence increasing the likelihood of higher sales) versus the costs of extending credit to customers (i.e., some customers may not pay us for the goods or services we provided to them).

To summarize, if a company extends credit to its customers then it will have accrued revenue transactions that give rise to the possibility of *uncollectible accounts receivable*. How we account and report for these uncollectible accounts is the focus of this chapter.

UNCOLLECTIBLE ACCOUNTS RECEIVABLE

Uncollectible accounts receivable are also known as *bad debts*. An overview of accounting for bad debts is provided in Figure 13.1.

WHEN TO RECOGNIZE BAD DEBTS?

The first decision point on Figure 13.1 coincides with the question, when should we recognize bad debts? The answer is obvious to most students—

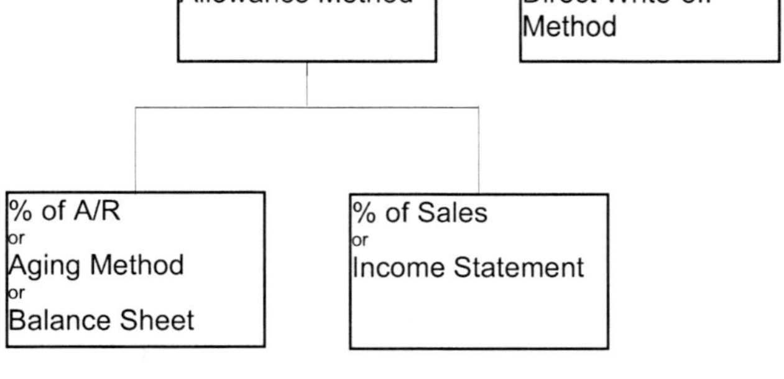

Figure 13.1. Accounting for Bad Debts.

when you determine that the customer will not pay you. This is referred to in Figure 13.1 as the *Direct Write-off Method.*

Using the Direct Write-off Method when it is determined that a customer will not pay all or part of their account receivable balance, we "*write-off*" their account by reducing Accounts Receivable. When an Asset no longer has future value it becomes an Expense so we will also record Bad Debt Expense which, like all Expenses, reduces Equity. *Recording Bad Debts Expense always has the effect of reducing Assets and reducing Equity.*

There is a problem with the Direct Write-off Method though. What if the credit sale is made in one accounting period, say, 20X1 and the bad debt is not recorded until a later accounting period, say, 20X2? It might be tempting to say you don't much care, but it brings us to an important concept underlying the accrual basis of accounting.

> The Matching Principle states that we should record all of the Expenses incurred to help us earn Revenue in the *same accounting period* as the related Revenue. Another way of thinking about this principle is that if we are going to report the good part of a transaction now (i.e., the Revenue or accomplishment) then we should also report the bad part of the transaction (i.e., the Expense or the cost of our efforts).

The Direct Write-off Method is inconsistent with The Matching Principle.

The *Allowance Method* of accounting for bad debts attempts to record the Expense associated with uncollectible accounts receivable in the same period as the related credit sale. If credit sales are made in 20X1, then an "*allowance*" or "*provision*" is made of the expected bad debts expense and it is also recorded in 20X1. By doing this, we say we have "matched" the Expense of extending credit (i.e., uncollectible accounts receivable) with the benefits of extending credit (i.e., increased credit sales).

The Allowance Method is consistent with The Matching Principle and is, therefore, required in Financial Accounting. The Allowance Method requires that we make an educated guess about what will happen in the future. We have to make an estimate as to what portion of our credit sales or accounts receivable will ultimately not be collected in the future. The Matching Principle would argue, however, that it is better to be "approximately correct rather than precisely wrong." That is, it is better to make an imperfect estimate of bad debts using the Allowance Method and record that expense in the same period as the credit sale, than to simply ignore the cost of bad debts until they almost inevitably occur at some point in the future.

Before we proceed with our discussion of the Allowance Method we need to introduce the concept of *Control Accounts* and *Subsidiary Ledgers.* A Control Account is one that contains an overall total for which more detail is provided in a Subsidiary Ledger. Accounts Receivable is a Control Account and the details about Accounts Receivable are provided in the Accounts Receivable Subsidiary Ledger.

You may think of the Accounts Receivable Subsidiary Ledger as a book with each page in the book representing information for a particular customer. The company's Control Account, Accounts Receivable, tells us how much it is owed by all of its customers combined. To determine how much a specific customer owes, we turn to the customer's page in the Accounts Receivable Subsidiary Ledger.

Hopefully it will make intuitive sense that if we add up the individual totals for each customer in the Accounts Receivable Subsidiary Ledger the grand total should equal the amount recorded in the Control Account, Accounts Receivable. From a bookkeeping standpoint what this means is that each time we change the Accounts Receivable account we must also post a change to one or more customers' pages in the Accounts Receivable Subsidiary Ledger. Proper posting ensures that the overall total reported in Accounts Receivable agrees with the summation of customer balances from all the pages in the Accounts Receivable Subsidiary Ledger.

Now, let's get back to recording bad debts using the Allowance Method. If we estimate that a certain portion of Accounts Receivable will not be collected in the future then we must reduce the Asset, Accounts Receivable, and record an Expense, Bad Debt Expense. After all, an Asset that no longer has any expected future value becomes an Expense. Using the Allowance Method we make an estimate of bad debts and record it, often as an adjusting entry, in the same period as the related credit sales.

There is just one problem. If we reduce the Accounts Receivable control account, whose page do we post this reduction to in the Accounts Receivable Subsidiary Ledger? At this point we are just estimating that we will not be able to collect the entire amount owed to us by all of our customers. However, we do not yet know which customer or customers will not pay.

To resolve this we resort to some bookkeeping gymnastics. We create a new account, called the *Allowance for Bad Debts,* which tags along with an existing account, Accounts Receivable, and reduces the asset without affecting the related Accounts Receivable Subsidiary Ledger. The Allowance for Bad Debts is referred to as a *contra-account,* meaning that it is an account that reduces the balance in another account. Importantly, *entries to a contra-account are not posted to any subsidiary ledger.*

Let's summarize this discussion to this point. Using the Allowance Method we record an estimate of bad debts in the same period as the related credit sales. *Remember, recording bad debts expense always has the effect of reducing Assets and reducing Equity.* The *way* that we record bad debts using the Allowance Method is by decreasing Assets with an entry to the Allowance for Bad Debts and by decreasing Equity with an entry to Bad Debts Expense.

THE ALLOWANCE METHOD: AN EXAMPLE

Let's assume we have five customers to whom we make credit sales of $100 each in 20X1. Our total credit sales would be $500, so we would increase Accounts Receivable by $500 and record Revenue of $500. We would also maintain an Accounts Receivable Subsidiary Ledger with five pages, one for each customer. Each page would show the customer's current account balance, contact information, credit history, and so forth. In this case, each customer has a current account balance of $100, and the combined total of the five pages equals the $500 balance in the control account, Accounts Receivable.

Now, let's assume that these receivables are all outstanding, or uncollected, at year end. Perhaps we know from past experience that a certain, hopefully small, portion of outstanding receivables never get paid. For our example, this amount will be 5% of outstanding receivables, or 5% times $500 (.05 * $500) equals $25. We are acknowledging that $25 out of $500 of Accounts Receivable will probably not be collected in the future even though we do not yet know for certain who is not going to pay us.

To record the estimated Bad Debt Expense we will create a contra-asset account, Allowance for Bad Debts. Since an entry to this account has the effect of reducing Assets, we will show the entry to that account with a negative sign. Table 13.2 shows how our example would look in workpaper format:

Table 13.2. Recording Bad Debt Expense Using the Allowance Method

	Accounts Receivable	*Allowance for Bad Debts*	*Sales*	*Bad Debts Expense*
Credit Sale	+ 500		+ 500	
Estimated Bad Debts		– 25		– 25

On The Income Statement we would report Sales of $500 and Bad Debt Expense of $25; note that we have matched the expense of credit sales with the revenue from the credit sales.

On The Balance Sheet, the accounts receivable might look like Table 13.3:

Table 13.3. Accounts Receivable on the Balance Sheet Using the Allowance Method

Accounts Receivable	$500
Less: Allowance for Bad Debts	25
Accounts Receivable, Net	$475

"Accounts Receivable, Net" means net of, or after deducting, the related Allowance for Bad Debts. Note that since we are still legally owed $500 we are reporting Accounts Receivable of $500 above. In our Accounts Receivable Subsidiary Ledger the totals of the individual customer pages will add up to $500 because we do not post the entry from the Allowance for Bad Debts account to the Accounts Receivable Subsidiary Ledger.

In essence, what the above reporting on the balance sheet says is,

> "Even though we are legally owed $500 by our customers, past experience, common sense, and prudence indicates that we will only collect $475 in the future so we have acknowledged this reality by recording a reduction to our Asset of $25 and a reduction to our Equity of $25."

What happens when we later realize an actual occurrence of an uncollectible account receivable of, say, $25? We then say that we "write-off" the specific customer's account balance with a "charge" to the Allowance for Bad Debts Account and reduce Accounts Receivable since we now know which specific customer(s) did not pay us. This is reflected in workpaper format in Table 13.4:

Table 13.4. Write-off of a Specific Customer's Bad Debt With the Allowance Method

	Accounts Receivable	*Allowance for Bad Debts*
Credit Sale	+ 500	
Estimated Bad Debts		– 25
Bad Debt is Realized	– 25	+ 25
Account Balances	+ 475	0

Let's note two things in the table above that are not obvious. First, when the bad debit is realized, no additional bad debt expense is recorded. Rather, we had already made an allowance, or provision, for this in the past and now we are simply dealing with the subsequent result.

Second, the "Accounts Receivable, Net" would be unchanged by the write-off of the $25 bad debt. How can this be? Recall that Accounting Receivable, Net is the total balance in Accounts Receivable minus the total balance in the Allowance for Bad Debts. Before the write-off of $25 the Accounting Receivable, Net would have been ($500 – $25) $475. After the write-off of $25 the Accounts Receivable, Net would be ($475 – $0) $475. This might seem odd and a bit counterintuitive but it is correct. This might be why we used the phrase bookkeeping gymnastics in an earlier paragraph.

SUMMARY

The Allowance Method records bad debt expense in the same period as the related credit sales. In doing so, it follows the matching principle and is required in Financial Accounting. Table 13.5 summarizes the main points from this chapter.

Table 13.5. Transaction Analysis Summary of Accounting for Bad Debts

Transaction	*Allowance Method*	*Direct Write-Off Method*
Consistent with The Matching Principle?	Yes Required in Financial Accounting	No **
Credit Sale	+ Asset (A/R) + Revenue	+ Asset (A/R) + Revenue
Estimated Bad Debt	– Asset (Allowance for Bad Debts) – Equity (Bad Debt Expense)	NONE – No estimate made.
Bad Debt is Realized	+ Asset (Allowance for Bad Debts) – Asset (A/R)	– Asset (A/R) – Equity (Bad Debt Expense)

** Although the Direct Write-off Method is prohibited in Financial Accounting it is discussed in this chapter for the following reason. It is the intuitively obvious choice for recording bad debts expense. If we don't mention it, a student will usually do so. We introduce this method, then, to acknowledge it and to highlight the fact that it is inconsistent with The Matching Principle.

CHAPTER 14

OPERATING ACTIVITIES

The Allowance Method for Bad Debts

INTRODUCTION

In Chapter 13 we learned that the Allowance Method is consistent with The Matching Principle and is required in Financial Accounting. In this chapter we will discuss how to estimate bad debts when using the Allowance Method.

UNCOLLECTIBLE ACCOUNTS RECEIVABLE

The overview of accounting for bad debts from Chapter 13 is reproduced in Figure 14.1 (next page) for your convenience.

Financial Accounting: A Course for All Majors, pp. 101–109

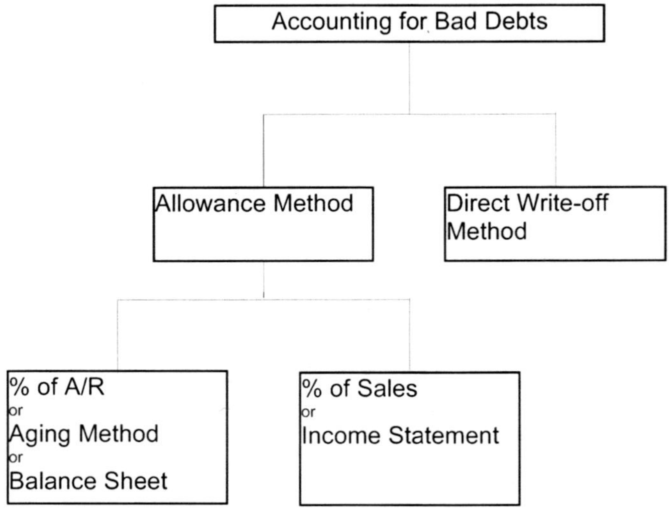

Figure 14.1. Accounting for Bad Debts.

THE ALLOWANCE METHOD: HOW TO ESTIMATE BAD DEBTS?

The Allowance Method records bad debt expense in the same period as the related credit sales. This is often before you know which specific customers are not going to pay their bills. However, we do know that credit sales cause bad debts so we try to match the Expense with the Revenue and record both in the same time period.

We might also have some idea of what level of bad debts we can expect. The best guide here is past experience adjusted for anticipated changes in the future. For example, if we have recently become more liberal with our credit policies and have been extending credit to more customers we would expect bad debts in the future to be higher than in the past. Or, if we believe economic conditions are deteriorating then we might also expect our bad debts to increase in the future.

As you can see in Figure 14.1 above, there are two approaches to estimated bad debt expense using the Allowance Method. One method is referred to as the Percentage of Accounts Receivable, Aging Method, or Balance Sheet Approach. The other is referred to as the Percentage of Sales or Income Statement Approach.

The two methods may not produce the same answer. Estimating bad debts is fraught with uncertainty because it involves an attempt to predict the future. These two methods are both valid, but they approach the issue from quite different perspectives.

EXAMPLE 1

The information in Table 14.1 will be used to illustrate the Income Statement and Balance Sheet Approaches in this chapter:

The last line in Table 14.1 requires some explanation. The Allowance for Bad Debts is a contra-asset account and *contra-asset accounts are permanent accounts,* meaning they are not closed, or zeroed out, at the end of each accounting period. The Allowance for Bad Debts account could have a nonzero balance—it could already have something in it from a prior period. The only reason the Allowance for Bad Debts would end each year with exactly zero is if our estimates of bad debt from prior periods were exactly equal to the actual bad debts we had subsequently realized; this is unrealistic, even in a textbook example. In Table 14.1, you can see that the Allowance for Bad Debts currently has a normal balance of $100.

There are two basic questions you need to be able to answer for this example. First, what is the estimated bad debt expense for 20X1? Second, what is the Accounts Receivable, Net after making the year end adjustment for bad debt expense? We will answer these questions first for the Income Statement Approach and then for the Balance Sheet Approach.

INCOME STATEMENT APPROACH

This method focuses its attention on an income statement account, Sales. Specifically, it poses the question, "What portion of our credit *sales* will be uncollectible?" For this example, we will assume that 5% of our credit sales are estimated to be uncollectible. We will then estimate bad debt expense by multiplying our total credit sales by 5% to get ($10,000 * .05) $500. Let's formalize this in Step 1 of Figure 14.2 (next page).

Now, what is the Accounts Receivable, Net after recording the bad debts expense for 20X1? To answer this question let's first determine what

Table 14.1. Accounting for Bad Debts Example—Example 1

Credit Sales During 20X1	$10,000
– Cash Collections During 20X1	6,000
= Outstanding Accounts Receivable, 12/31/X1	$4,000
Normal Balance** in Allowance for Bad Debts	$100

** To avoid confusion in this course, we do not cover the case of a debit, or deficit, balance in the Allowance for Bad Debts.

Step 1: Bad Debt Expense $_{\text{IS Approach}}$ = Total Credit Sales * Estimated % Bad Debts

Step 2: Balance in Allowance = Normal Balance + Bad Debt Expense $_{\text{IS Approach}}$

Figure 14.2. Accounting for Bad Debts Using the Income Statement Approach.

amount would be in the Allowance for Bad Debts by using the formula in Step 2 of Figure 14.2. This tells us to take our result from Step 1, $500, and add it to the existing, normal balance in the Allowance account, $100, to get the current account balance in the Allowance account, $600.

The Accounts Receivable, Net is the outstanding Accounts Receivable minus the balance in the Allowance for Bad Debts, which is shown in Table 14.2:

Table 14.2. Net Accounts Receivable Using the Income Statement Approach

Outstanding Accounts Receivable, 12/31/X1	$4,000
Less: Allowance for Bad Debts	600
Equals: Accounts Receivable, Net	$3,400

When using the Income Statement Approach you need to follow this same sequence. First determine the bad debt expense for the current period (Step 1), then use this amount to determine the new balance in the Allowance for Bad Debts account (Step 2).

THE BALANCE SHEET APPROACH

This method focuses its attention on a balance sheet account, Accounts Receivable. Specifically, it poses the question, "What portion of our outstanding *accounts receivable* will be uncollectible?" In our example we have $4,000 of outstanding accounts receivable on 12/31/X1 so we will try to estimate what portion of this amount will be uncollectible.

The Balance Sheet Approach typically uses an Aging Schedule to make its estimate of bad debt. Table 14.3 is the Aging Schedule for this example. Table 14.3 divides the outstanding accounts receivable into categories based upon how long it has been since the related credit sales were made. This is referred to as "aging" the receivables. Note the consistency in our

Table 14.3. Aging Schedule for the Balance Sheet Approach to Estimating Bad Debts Expense—Example 1

(1) *Aging Category*	*(2)* *Outstanding Accounts Receivable*	*(3)* *Percent Uncollectible*	*(2) * (3) = (4)* *Amount Uncollectible*
0–30 Days	$1,000	.05	$50
31–90 Days	1,500	.10	150
Over 90 Days	1,500	.20	300
Total	$4,000		$500

example in that the summation of the three categories equals the outstanding accounts receivable of $4,000.

Let's assume that the agreed upon credit terms between the seller and buyer were that the buyer would pay the entire balance of their account within 30 days of the sale date. In the table above, $1,000 of the outstanding accounts receivable are within the agreed upon 30 days so they are not past due. The next line shows that $1,500 of outstanding accounts receivable are related to sales that were made somewhere between 31 and 90 days ago. These accounts are all past due. Finally, we have another $1,500 of receivables related to sales made more than 90 days ago.

The intuition behind the Aging Schedule is that we would expect the probability of trouble to increase with the age of the account. That is, the risk of bad debts increases with the age of the account.

In Table 14.3, column 3 reflects our estimates of what portion of each category of receivables will be uncollectible. This column reflects the intuition that older accounts are more likely to be uncollectible, hence we see the percentages increasing from 5, to 10, to 20%, respectively, for the three categories of receivables. Column 4 is calculated by multiplying column 2 by column 3. You should verify our calculations of column 4 and be able to complete this portion of an Aging Schedule.

Now, focus on the last line. In column 2, we have totaled the three categories of receivables and we merely note that the total agrees with the $4,000 of outstanding accounts receivable in our example. The total in column 4, $500, reflects the portion of the $4,000 that we are predicting will be uncollectible. If our estimates prove true, then we will collect ($4,000 – $500) $3,500 of the accounts receivable and we will have to "write-off" the remaining $500 of accounts receivable as bad debts.

We are going to answer the same two questions as before but in reverse order. What is the Accounts Receivable, Net after the adjustment for bad debts expense? The answer will come directly from the Aging Schedule as shown in Step A of Figure 14.3:

Step A: Desired Balance in Allowance = Uncollectible Amount from Aging Schedule

Step B: Bad Debt Exp. $_{\text{BS Approach}}$ = Desired Bal. in Allowance – Normal Bal. in Allowance

Figure 14.3. Accounting for Bad Debts Using the Balance Sheet Approach.

So, our Accounts Receivable, Net is the total outstanding receivables minus the desired balance in the Allowance account, as shown in Table 14.4:

Table 14.4. Net Accounts Receivable Using the Balance Sheet Approach

Outstanding Accounts Receivable, 12/31/X1	$4,000
Less: Allowance for Bad Debts	500
Equals: Accounts Receivable, Net	$3,500

Now, our second question is what is the bad debt expense for 20X1? To answer this question we will use the formula in Step B of Figure 14.3. It tells us to take our result from Step A, $500, subtract the existing, normal balance in the Allowance account, $100, and our answer is $400. Using the Balance Sheet Approach the bad debt expense is the amount that forces the balance in the Allowance account to equal the uncollectible amount of $500 derived from the Aging Schedule.

When using the Balance Sheet Approach you need to follow this same sequence. First determine the new balance in the Allowance for Bad Debts Account (Step A), then use this amount to determine the bad debts expense (Step B).

Table 14.5 summarizes this example with a side-by-side comparison of our results. We hope this will be useful to quickly review the example from this chapter.

EXAMPLE 2

This is a challenging topic. Most students cannot fully appreciate the subtle differences between the Income Statement and Balance Sheet

Table 14.5. Comparison of Accounting for Bad Debts With the Income Statement and Balance Sheet Approaches—Example 1

Income Statement Approach		*Balance Sheet Approach*	
Step 1:		**Step A:**	
Bad debt expense = ($10,000 * .05)	$500	Outstanding Accounts Receivable	$4,000
		– Allowance (from Aging)	500
		= Accounts Receivable, Net	$3,500
Step 2:			
Outstanding Accounts Receivable	$4,000	**Step B:**	
– Allowance ($100 Beg. Bal. + $500 above)	600	Bad debt expense =	
= Accounts Receivable, Net	$3,400	$500 from Aging – $100 Beg. Bal. =	$400

Approaches until they work through a problem on their own. Consider the information in Table 14.6:

Table 14.6. Accounting for Bad Debts—Example 2

Credit Sales During 20X1	$100,000
Cash Collections During 20X1	85,000
Normal Balance in Allowance for Bad Debts	200

For the Income Statement Approach we will assume 3.5% of credit sales are uncollectible. For the Balance Sheet Approach we assume the Aging Schedule in Table 14.7:

Table 14.7. Aging Schedule for the Balance Sheet Approach to Estimating Bad Debts Expense—Example 2

(1) Aging Category	*(2) Accounts Receivable*	*(3) Percent Uncollectible*
0–30 Days	$4,000	.10
31–90 Days	5,000	.20
Over 90 Days	6,000	.30
Total	$15,000	

For each method, what is the bad debt expense for 20X1 and what is the Accounts Receivable, Net after the adjustment is made for bad debt expense? Remember to follow the sequence given in this chapter for each method. The answers are reported at the end of this chapter.

SUMMARY

Estimating bad debt expense is rather complicated from a technical standpoint because there are two methods that may be used to accomplish this task. Each method is valid, but approaches the task from a different perspective. We have tried to clearly delineate the different approaches, but the fact remains that it is always more difficult to learn two methods rather than only one method.

This concludes our discussion of uncollectible accounts and bad debts expense. This is a very technical topic. Chapter 15 should be a nice break because it is a very conceptual chapter. Until then, work through the example above on your own, check your answers with those reported below, and then work through it again on your own. Repeat this cycle until you start to get comfortable with the two methods discussed in this chapter.

SOLUTION TO EXAMPLE 2—INCOME STATEMENT APPROACH

For the Income Statement Approach we will assume 3.5% of credit sales are uncollectible. In Step 1 using the *Income Statement Approach* the estimated bad debt expense is always the credit sales multiplied by the percent of sales uncollectible. Any balance in the Allowance account may be ignored in determining the bad debt expense. What is the estimated amount of bad debt expense for 20X1 using the Income Statement Approach? Answer: **($100,000 * .035) $3,500.**

In Step 2 using the *Income Statement Approach* the ending balance in the Allowance for Bad Debts is always the existing, normal balance ($200) plus the estimated bad debt expense from Step 1 ($3,500), a total of $3,700. What is the Accounts Receivable, Net at year end 20X1 using the Income Statement Approach? The Accounts Receivable, Net at year end 20X1 is the Outstanding Accounts Receivable at year end 20X1 ($15,000) minus the balance in the Allowance for Bad Debts after the adjustment in Step 1 ($3,700), or $11,300.

SOLUTION TO EXAMPLE 2—BALANCE SHEET APPROACH

In Step A using the *Balance Sheet Approach* the desired ending balance in the Allowance for Bad Debts is always the amount derived from the aging schedule, $3,200, which is shown in Table 14.8:

Table 14.8. Completed Aging Schedule for the Balance Sheet Approach to Estimating Bad Debts Expense—Example 2

(1) Aging Category	*(2) Outstanding Accounts Receivable*	*(3) Percent Uncollectible*	*(2) * (3) = (4) Amount Uncollectible*
0–30 Days	$4,000	.10	$400
31–90 Days	5,000	.20	1,000
Over 90 Days	6,000	.30	1,800
Total	$15,000		$3,200

What is the Accounts Receivable, Net at year end 20X1 using the Balance Sheet Approach? The Outstanding Accounts Receivable at year end 20X1 ($15,000) minus the desired ending balance in the Allowance for Bad Debts from Step A ($3,200), or $11,800.

In Step B using the *Balance Sheet Approach* the estimated bad debt expense is always the desired ending balance in the Allowance account derived from the aging schedule minus the existing, normal balance in that account. What is the estimated amount of bad debt expense for 20X1 using the Balance Sheet Approach? Answer: **($3,200 - $200) $3,000.**

To summarize, Table 14.9 provides a comparison of the two solutions for your review.

Table 14.9. Comparison of Accounting for Bad Debts With the Income Statement and Balance Sheet Approaches—Example 2

Income Statement Approach		*Balance Sheet Approach*	
Step 1:		**Step A:**	
Bad debt expense = ($100,000 * .035)	$$3,500	Outstanding Accounts Receivable =	$15,000
		– Allowance (from Aging)	3,200
		= Accounts Receivable, Net	$11,800
Step 2:			
Outstanding Accounts Receivable =	$15,000	**Step B:**	
– Allowance ($200 Beg. Bal. + $3,500 above)	3,700	Bad debt expense =	
= Accounts Receivable, Net	$11,300	$3,200 from Aging – $0 Beg. Bal. =	$3,200

CHAPTER 15

OPERATING ACTIVITIES

The Revenue Recognition Principle

INTRODUCTION

Chapters 13 and 14 have focused on the problem of uncollectible accounts. This chapter will conclude our discussion of revenue transactions.

OPERATING ACTIVITIES: REVENUE TRANSACTIONS REVISITED

At this point, one has to wonder if there is anything more to revenue transactions than accounting for bad debts. Actually, we have yet to cover the most important issue surrounding revenue transactions. The most important issue surrounding revenue transactions is the broader, conceptual issue of *when* revenue should be recognized. We refer to this more formally as the Revenue Recognition Principle.

The Revenue Recognition Principle states that we should recognize revenue when the (1) seller has provided a good or service to a buyer in exchange for the (2) buyer's payment, or realistically collectible promise of payment, and (3) that substantially all of the risks and benefits of ownership have been transferred from the seller to the buyer.

Financial Accounting: A Course for All Majors, pp. 111–118

Condition 1 says the seller has satisfied their part of the deal by providing a good or service. Consider the following situation regarding condition 1. What if the seller has promised to provide a good or service, has the capability to do so, but will not deliver the good or service until some point in the future? The Revenue Recognition Principle says we should not anticipate what the seller will do in the future, but rather we should wait to recognize revenue until the seller has actually delivered the goods or services.

Condition 2 says the buyer has satisfied their part of the deal by either already paying for the goods or services, or agreeing to do so in the future. We made up a new term, "realistically collectible", in the definition above. Consider the following situation regarding condition 2. What if the buyer's credit history is terrible? What if we extend credit to customers that cannot get financing elsewhere and do not appear to have any financial capacity to pay us? We may have a legal claim against the customer, but do we really have a "realistically collectible" account receivable? The answer could be "no," and if so we should not recognize revenue because condition 2 has not been met.

Condition 3 exists because enterprising, perhaps you could say conniving, individuals have devised means to seemingly satisfy conditions 1 and 2, yet a reasonable person might easily conclude that a legitimate transaction has not occurred. Consider the following situations involving condition 3. What if the seller has delivered goods to the buyer, but the buyer has the right to return all of the goods to the seller for an unconditional refund at any time in the next, say, 6 months? Furthermore, the buyer is not obligated to pay the seller until she has decided to keep the goods. What if the seller has delivered goods to the buyer, but the seller has agreed to provide critical installation services for the buyer and the seller has not yet provided these services? Furthermore, the agreement states that if the buyer is not unconditionally satisfied with the installation services, she may return the goods for a complete refund.

The overall point of The Revenue Recognition Principle is really that a legitimate exchange transaction has occurred between a buyer and a seller and that there is no reason to doubt both parties will honor their side of the agreement. In essence, it is what some might call a "done deal."

Now, since we've covered accounting for bad debts we know that sometimes we record credit sales only to find out later that some people could not or would not pay us. Does this violate The Revenue Recognition Principle? This is a difficult question and it takes a bit of finesse to answer it. The Revenue Recognition Principle does not say that we have to know the future with certainty. It does say that we should evaluate all the circumstances known to us at the *time of sale* and make a *reasonable judgment* about whether the transaction is, or is not, a "done deal." When we make credit sales, we do so in good faith and with the implicit assumption that the other party is acting in good faith too. As the future unfolds, things may change and the buyer or seller may not be able to honor their previous agreement, but the point is that a *reasonable person* would have concluded at the *time of sale* that this was a "done deal" and that at the *time of sale* both parties were acting in good faith.

In addition, The Matching Principle says that if we can realistically expect to incur costs associated with the revenue, then we should go ahead and record the expense at the same time that we record the revenue. In essence, The Matching Principle says you cannot record the good part of the transaction without also recognizing the bad part of the transaction. When we make credit sales, we generally know, given the law of averages, that some portion of these sales will be uncollectible. We do not know which specific customers will not pay us so we typically record the revenue on all the sales transactions. However, we also record a good faith estimate of the future cost we will incur when we realize losses from bad debts.

THE WHY QUESTION

Why all the fuss over The Revenue Recognition Principle? Unfortunately, one of the most common means by which people perpetrate fraud in financial statements is by prematurely or illegitimately recognizing revenue; in short, *they claim more revenue than they should in an effort to attain some financial benefit.*

Notice that we said "people" in the statement above. Companies do not commit fraud, people do; organizations do not commit fraud, people do; governments do not commit fraud, people do. When two or more people are acting together, it is tempting to say that the "organization" or the "company" committed fraud, but these entities are just collections of people and the people are the ones who are ultimately responsible for their actions. *At the end of the day, financial statements are only as credible as the people that have produced them.* If you don't trust the people, why would you trust their accounting or their financial statements?

SALES RETURNS

What about sales returns? Condition 3 above might be interpreted to mean that a seller cannot recognize revenue until we know with certainty that a buyer will not change their mind and return their purchase. Or, we could approach this like we do with bad debts and if we're going to record the revenue from the sale then we should also anticipate returns associated with the sales and record those anticipated returns in the same period the revenue is recognized.

For most consumer transactions, sales made with the right of return are recorded as sales based upon the implicit assumption that the customer will keep the merchandise. If the customer does return the goods for a refund, the business records this as a *reduction in revenue, not an expense.* What is the label for an account which reduces another account? The term is "contra" and in this case we use a *contra-revenue account called Sales Returns.*

Let's say Big Box Retailer sells a total of $10,000 worth of merchandise to numerous customers. For simplicity, we'll assume these were all cash sales. Later, several customers return items for refunds of, say, $500. What is the retailer's Sales for the period? Did the retailer have Sales of $10,000 with an Expense of $500, or did the retailer have "true" Sales of $9,500? Typical accounting treatment is the latter, and we use the term Net Sales to report the total Sales minus the Sales Returns.

Sales minus Sales Returns = Net Sales

Table 15.1 shows how these transactions would be recorded:

Table 15.1. Recording Sales Returns

	Operating Cash	*Sales*	*Sales Returns*
Initial Sale	+ 10,000	+ 10,000	
Returns	– 500		– 500
Totals	+ 9,500	+ 10,000	– 500

On the retailer's income statement for the period, the first item at the top of their income statement might appear as shown in Table 15.2:

Table 15.2. Reporting Net Sales on the Income Statement

Sales	$10,000
Less: Sales Returns	500
Net Sales or Sales, Net	$9,500

Actually, most published income statements simply start off with Net Sales, with the understanding that the reader knows what this number represents.

What if the Sales occur in one period, but the anticipated Sales Returns will not occur until the next accounting period? Doesn't this violate the matching principle? The answer is yes, but this can be resolved. If a retailer makes a large amount of Sales in, say, December and their year end is December 31st, then they need to record an estimate of their anticipated Sales Returns, similar in concept to how we recorded an estimate of future bad debts. A major difference is that *bad debts is treated as an expense, while sales returns is a contra-revenue account.*

SCENARIOS INVOLVING REVENUE RECOGNITION

Let's conclude this chapter with an exercise. For each scenario below, indicate whether the firm's action with respect to revenue recognition was acceptable. The answers are reported at the end of this chapter.

1. A firm records revenue in 20X1 so that employees can get their Christmas bonuses, which were based upon achieving a certain level of sales. The related products will not be shipped to the customers until early in 20X2.
2. A company has received payment from the customer so they record revenue in 20X1 even though they will not provide the good or service until 20X2.
3. A company records revenue in 20X1 because the buyer has signed a contract to buy the company's goods. The goods will be delivered in 20X2.
4. A company is desperate to meet a sales target so they ship some product to a customer that has horrible credit and has not paid the firm for the last three orders.
5. A company is desperate to meet a sales target so they ship some products to an established customer with excellent credit history. The customer did not order the goods, however.
6. A company sells a product on credit to an established customer with an excellent credit history in 20X1. Since they had already met their sales targets for 20X1, and they will not get any further bonus for exceeding that target, they decide to wait until 20X2 to record the sales.
7. A company's sales team is determined to meet their sales quota for the year. They convince some customers to accept shipments of goods in 20X1 because they promised them that they can return anything they don't want or need, at no expense to the customer, in 20X2.

8. A company makes sales on credit knowing full well that some customers probably will not pay their bills. They go ahead and record the revenue from the credit sales but also record an estimated bad debt expense.
9. A retailer makes a huge amount of cash sales during the holiday season and records the sales as revenue immediately. They have a very liberal return policy and expect about 5% of the stuff to be returned for a cash refund so they record an estimated sales return equal to 5% of their total sales.
10. A company ships products to the president's home address and records the shipments as sales in 20X1 so that the company's bank will be impressed and renew a loan with the company. In 20X2, the company president will return the goods and the accounts receivable will simply be taken off the books.

SUMMARY

Chapters 13, 14, and 15 have covered the basic revenue transactions associated with the operating activities of an organization. You should review the answers to the revenue recognition scenarios reported below before moving to Chapter 16.

SCENARIOS INVOLVING REVENUE RECOGNITION—SOLUTIONS

For each scenario below, indicate whether the firm's action with respect to revenue recognition was acceptable.

1. A firm records revenue in 20X1 so that employees can get their Christmas bonuses, which were based upon achieving a certain level of sales. The related products will not be shipped to the customers until early in 20X2. Answer: Revenue should not be recognized until the products are shipped in 20X2.
2. A company has received payment from the customer so they record revenue in 20X1 even though they will not provide the good or service until 20X2. Answer: When a customer pays in advance, we should record Unearned Revenue. The Revenue should not be recorded until the product is shipped in 20X2.
3. A company records revenue in 20X1 because the buyer has signed a contract to buy the company's goods. The goods will be delivered in 20X2. Answer: Although the customer's contract to buy goods

from the company is an important economic event, Revenue would not be recognized in the Financial Accounting records when the contract is signed because the company has not yet delivered the goods. When they deliver the goods in 20X2 it would be appropriate to recognize Revenue.

4. A company is desperate to meet a sales target so they ship some product to a customer that has horrible credit and has not paid the firm for the last three orders. Answer: Since the likelihood of this credit sale resulting in a collectible Account Receivable seems quite low, this is not a legitimate Revenue transaction. Actually, it's just stupid, but people sometimes do stupid things (i.e., things that make no economic sense for the organization) when they are chasing personal financial benefits.
5. A company is desperate to meet a sales target so they ship some products to an established customer with excellent credit history. The customer did not order the goods, however. Answer: If the customer did not order the goods then there is a very high likelihood that she will return them for a refund. Consequently, Revenue should not be recognized.
6. A company sells a product on credit to an established customer with an excellent credit history in 20X1. Since they had already met their sales targets for 20X1, and they will not get any further bonus for exceeding that target, they decide to wait until 20X2 to record the sales. Answer: Revenue recognition issues usually deal with companies wanting to recognize Revenue prematurely so that they can impress someone and attain some financial benefit. In this case the company is delaying the recognition of Revenue. The Revenue Recognition Principle is not concerned with what period would best serve the personal financial interests of the people involved, but rather with recording Revenue in the time period in which the sale was actually completed. In this case the Revenue should be recognized in 20X1.
7. A company's sales team is determined to meet their sales quota for the year. They convince some customers to accept shipments of goods in 20X1 because they promised them that they can return anything they don't want or need, at no expense to the customer, in 20X2. Answer: Reasonable people might disagree on this one. We would argue for one of two alternatives. First, since the customers did not want the goods it is likely the goods will be returned so we should not recognize Revenue. Second, the sales team will argue that it always takes a bit of convincing to get customers to buy things so they will not like our first answer. We might consider

recognizing Revenue if and only if we also recorded a substantial, estimated sales return (a contra-revenue) to account for the expected returns. In the real world, the challenge in Financial Accounting is often in cases like this where the answer is not as clear as we would like it to be for classroom purposes!

8. A company makes sales on credit knowing full well that some customers probably will not pay their bills. They go ahead and record the revenue from the credit sales but also record an estimated bad debt expense. Answer: When a firm makes credit sales it is likely that some customers will not pay their bills. In Chapters 13 and 14 we learned that is acceptable to recognize Revenue as long as you follow The Matching Principle and also record an estimated bad debts expense.
9. A retailer makes a huge amount of cash sales during the holiday season and records the sales as revenue immediately. However, the company has a very liberal return policy and expects about 5% of the stuff to be returned for a cash refund. Answer: This chapter discussed sales returns. Since the company seems to have a good estimate of sales returns they should record Revenue but also record an estimate of sales returns (a contra-revenue) equal to 5% of the total holiday sales.
10. A company ships products to the president's home address and records the shipments as sales in 20X1 so that the company's bank will be impressed and renew a loan with the company. In 20X2, the company president will return the goods and the accounts receivable simply taken off the books. Answer: This is clearly a fraudulent transaction designed to dupe the company's bank into making a loan that they otherwise might not make. Revenue should not be recognized on this sham transaction.

CHAPTER 16

OPERATING ACTIVITIES

Inventory, Part I

INTRODUCTION

Chapters 13–15 covered some key issues involved in an entity's revenue cycle. Chapters 16 and 17 will focus on the expense cycle with an emphasis on inventory transactions.

OPERATING ACTIVITIES: EXPENSE TRANSACTIONS

Let's begin with a refresher on some basic expense transactions.

- Cash Transaction—A company receives a good or service from a vendor and simultaneously pays cash for the item: Operating Cash Flow decreases and Equity decreases via the recording of an Expense.
- Deferred Expense—A company pays cash today in exchange for something of value that they will not consume or sell until sometime in the future. Upon receipt of the goods or services, Assets (e.g., Supplies, Merchandise Inventory, Prepaid Items) increase to

Financial Accounting: A Course for All Majors, pp. 119–129

represent the value received and Assets (Operating Cash Flow) decrease for the amount of the payment. When the Asset is consumed or sold the Asset becomes an Expense so Assets are decreased and Equity is decreased by recording an Expense.

- Accrued Expense—A company receives a good or service from a vendor today in exchange for the company's promise to pay the vendor in the future; this is commonly referred to as a "charge", or "credit" purchase. The vendor is extending "credit" to our company. Using the accrual basis of accounting we recognize the transaction with an increase to Liabilities (e.g., some form of Payable) and a decrease to Equity via the recording of an Expense. When we later pay the vendor, we reduce Assets (Operating Cash Flow) and reduce Liabilities to reflect the payment of the obligation.

Table 16.1 summarizes the effects of these three basic transactions:

Table 16.1. Summary of Basic Expense Transactions

Transaction	*Before*	*Goods / Services Consumed or Sold*	*After*
Cash Purchase	N/A	– Op. Cash Flow – Equity (Expense)	N/A
Deferred Expense	– Op. Cash Flow + Assets	– Assets – Equity (Expense)	N/A
Accrued Expense	N/A	+ Liabilities (Payable) – Equity (Expense)	– Liabilities (Payable) – Op. Cash Flow

In Table 16.1, note that *Expense is recognized at the same point in all three transactions—when the goods or services are consumed or sold.* The difference among the three types of transactions is when the company pays for the good or service relative to when they consume or sell the related item.

DEFERRED EXPENSES: MERCHANDISE INVENTORY TRANSACTIONS

Accounting for Prepaid items like rent or insurance was covered during the discussion of adjustments and for the sake of brevity will not be repeated here. Our focus in this chapter will be on accounting for inventory transactions, which are a special case of deferred expenses.

Let's begin with a brief example and some definitions. Assume we are dealing with a merchandising business that buys goods, marks up their price, and resells the goods to customers. When they buy the goods they decrease Operating Cash Flow and increase Merchandise Inventory. When they later sell the merchandise, they do two things:

1. First, they record the amount received from the customer as an increase to Assets (Cash or Accounts Receivable) and an increase to Equity (Sales).
2. Second, since we've recorded the Revenue side of the transaction The Matching Principle dictates that we must also record the cost associated with the sale, namely the cost of the goods we sold to the customer. To do this, we reduce Merchandise Inventory for the cost of the goods sold and reduce Equity by recording an Expense called Cost of Goods Sold.

Example 1. Assume a merchandising company buys one unit of inventory costing $60 for cash. Next, assume the business prices the item for sale at, say, $100 and a customer buys it. Table 16.2 shows how these transactions would be recorded:

Table 16.2. Record the Purchase and Sale of Inventory—Example 1

	Operating Cash Flow	*Merchandise Inventory*	*Revenue / Sales*	*Expense / Cost of Goods Sold*
Purchase	– 60	+ 60		
Sale—Part 1	+100		+100	
Sale—Part 2		– 60		– 60
Subtotals	**+ 40**	**0**	**+100**	**– 60**

In Sale—Part 1 we have recorded the sale of the inventory to the customer for $100 cash. This transaction increases Sales and increases Operating Cash Flow. In Sale—Part 2 we have recorded the cost of what we sold as an Expense. The company did not "make" $100 on the sale to the customer. The business received $100 cash from the customer, but the item sold cost the business $60 so we need to record that cost as an Expense. We will call the Expense associated with inventory sold to customers, *Cost of Goods Sold (COGS)*.

The subtotals reflect Sales $100, Cost of Goods Sold $40, and the difference between the two would be our Gross Profit of $40. We sold our only unit of Merchandise Inventory so that account has a zero balance, and Operating Cash Flow contains the $40 of Gross Profit on the transaction.

Sales – Cost of Goods Sold = Gross Profit

Example 2. Assume a merchandising company buys *two* units of inventory costing $60 each and pays cash for them. Next, assume the business prices the items for sale at, say, $100 and a customer buys *one* of them. These transactions are recorded in Table 16.3.

Table 16.3. Recording the Purchase and Sale of Inventory—Example 2

	Operating Cash Flow	*Merchandise Inventory*	*Revenue / Sales*	*Expense / Cost of Goods Sold*
Purchase	– 120	+ 120		
Sale—Part 1	+100		+100	
Sale—Part 2		– 60		– 60
Subtotals	– 20	+ 60	+100	– 60

In Sale—Part 1 we have recorded the sale of one unit of inventory to the customer for $100 cash. In Sale—Part 2 we have recorded the cost of what we sold as an Expense. Since we only sold one of the two items we record, or match, only the cost of the one item sold with the Revenue from the sale.

If we look at the subtotals things are a bit more confusing in this example. In the two right-hand columns we are still reporting Sales of $100 and Cost of Goods Sold of $60, or Gross Profit of $40. This is the same as Example 1. However, in Example 2 we still have one unit of inventory in our possession so this account will have a balance equal to the cost of that unit of inventory, $60. That unit will presumably be sold in the future. Finally, the Operating Cash Flow reflects a negative $20 because we paid $120 cash for two units of inventory and thus far have only sold one unit for $100.

Not to digress too much, but there is an important lesson here. A business can be profitable in the sense of its revenues exceeding its expenses, but still have a shortage of cash. In this example, it took $120 cash to buy the inventory and even though we were able to sell one unit of inventory at a reasonable gross profit, we have still not recovered the entire cost of our inventory. *The mismatch between when a company receives cash from its customers for goods or services and when it has to pay for its own goods and services is referred to as The Cash Flow Problem.* This is what owners mean when they lament that they "are profitable, but are having trouble managing their cash flow." In a personal sense it's a bit like your bills being due on Monday when you won't get paid until the following Friday—you'll have what you need (hopefully!) on Friday, but that doesn't put cash into your checking account to pay the bills the preceding Monday.

THE INVENTORY EQUATION

Let's define *The Inventory Equation*:

Beginning Inventory + Purchases = Ending Inventory + Cost of Goods Sold

Beginning Inventory is what you "have on the shelf" in inventory at the beginning of the accounting period. Let's assume our Beginning Inventory in Example 2 is zero. Purchases represent the cost of the inventory acquired during the accounting period. In our example, this was two units at $60 each, or a total of $120. Ending Inventory is what we still have on hand at the end of the accounting period, one unit at a cost of $60. Finally, Cost of Goods Sold represents the cost of items sold to customers during the accounting period, one unit at a cost of $60.

The Inventory Equation can be expressed in either units of currency, as in Table 16.4:

Table 16.4. The Inventory Equation Expressed in Units of Currency

Beginning Inventory +	*Purchases*	=	*Ending Inventory +*	*Cost of Goods Sold*
$0	$120		$60	$60

Or, in physical units of inventory, as in Table 16.5:

Table 16.5. The Inventory Equation Expressed in Units of Inventory

Beginning Inventory +	*Purchases*	=	*Ending Inventory +*	*Cost of Goods Sold*
0	2		1	1

There are some key points to note about The Inventory Equation. The left-hand side is what we have – what we started with plus what we bought. It is also referred to as *Cost of Goods Available for Sale (COGAS)*:

Beginning Inventory + Purchases = Cost of Goods Available for Sale

The right-hand side is where it went – we either still have it (an Asset called Merchandise Inventory reflected in the equation as Ending Inventory) or it's gone (an Expense called Cost of Goods Sold).

The other point you should recognize about The Inventory Equation is that it can be rearranged just like any algebraic equation. This leads to the

Alternative Representation Number 1:

Beginning Inventory + Purchases – Ending Inventory = COGS

or, substituting for COGAS

COGAS – Ending Inventory = COGS

Alternative Representation Number 2:

Beginning Inventory + Purchases – COGS = Ending Inventory

or, substituting for COGAS

COGAS – COGS = Ending Inventory

Figure 16.1. Alternative Representations of the Inventory Equation.

following alternative representations of The Inventory Equation in Figure 16.1.

The thing to note about these alternative representations is that if you know three of the four variables in the equation you can always solve for the fourth. So, if you know Beginning Inventory, Purchases, and Ending Inventory then you can solve for COGS. Or, if you know Beginning Inventory, Purchases, and COGS then you can solve for Ending Inventory. This tiny bit of algebra is often useful when solving inventory problems.

The Allocation Challenge

Let's conclude this chapter with another example. In Example 3 the company buys one unit of inventory for $30. Later they buy a second unit of inventory for $90. They sell one unit of inventory for $100. What is their Cost of Goods Sold? Ending Inventory?

The purchases and the revenue side of the sale transactions are recorded in Table 16.6:

Table 16.6. Recording the Purchases and Sale of Inventory—Example 3

	Operating Cash Flow	*Merchandise Inventory*	*Revenue / Sales*	*Expense / Cost of Goods Sold*
Purchase 1	– 30	+ 30		
Purchase 2	– 90	+ 90		

Table continues on next page.

Table 16.6. Continued

	Operating Cash Flow	*Merchandise Inventory*	*Revenue / Sales*	*Expense / Cost of Goods Sold*
Sale—Part 1	+ 100		+ 100	
Sale—Part 2		?		?
Subtotals	**– 20**	**?**	**+100**	**?**

The challenge is to determine what to record for the Sale—Part 2. What portion of the amount in Merchandise Inventory should be charged to Cost of Goods Sold? In terms of physical units, we know that one unit was sold and that one unit remains in ending inventory, as shown in Table 16.7:

Table 16.7. Allocating Physical Units of Inventory in Example 3

Beginning Inventory +	*Purchases*	=	*Ending Inventory +*	*Cost of Goods Sold*
0	2		1	1

The answer is not so clear with respect to the units of currency that should be allocated to Cost of Goods Sold and Merchandise Inventory? Table 16.8 illustrates this problem. At this point, just start thinking about some potential answers. If you need to make an assumption to arrive at an answer, do it.

Table 16.8. Allocating Units of Currency in Example 3

Beginning Inventory +	*Purchases*	=	*Ending Inventory +*	*Cost of Goods Sold*
$0	$120		$?	$?

We will continue by listing four possible assumptions one could make to answer this question. Assumption 1: What if the first unit we purchased was the first unit we sold? This would mean that the second unit we purchased would be the unit still in ending inventory. Answer 1: If this assumption is valid then we get the answers shown in Table 16.9 for COGS and Ending Inventory.

Table 16.9. FIFO Cost Flow Assumption

A. Units of Currency

Beginning Inventory +	*Purchases*	=	*Ending Inventory* +	*Cost of Goods Sold*
$0	$120		$90	$30

B. Recorded Transactions, Cost of Goods Sold, and Ending Merchandise Inventory

	Operating Cash Flow	*Merchandise Inventory*	*Revenue / Sales*	*Expense / Cost of Goods Sold*
Purchase 1	– 30	+ 30		
Purchase 2	– 90	+ 90		
Sale—Part 1	+ 100		+ 100	
Sale—Part 2		– 30		– 30
Subtotals	**– 20**	**+ 90**	**+ 100**	**– 30**

This method and assumption is referred to as *First-In, First-Out, abbreviated FIFO.* Notice that the acronym refers to the assumption we are making to determine Cost of Goods Sold. And, once we've determine COGS then we could determine Ending Inventory by subtraction. That is, $0 + $120 – $30 = Ending Inventory.

FIFO implies Last-In, Still Here, or LISH. LISH refers to the assumption we are making about Ending Inventory. Once we've determined Ending Inventory we could determine COGS by subtraction. That is, $0 + $120 – $90 = Cost of Goods Sold. These are just two different ways to solve the same problem. *For more complex inventory problems it is often best to determine Ending Inventory first, then solve for COGS by subtraction.*

Assumption 2: What if the last unit we purchased was the first unit we sold? This would mean that the first unit we purchased would be the unit still in ending inventory. Answer 1: If this assumption is valid then we get the answers shown in Table 16.10 for COGS and Ending Inventory.

Table 16.10. LIFO Cost Flow Assumption

A. Units of Currency:

Beginning Inventory +	*Purchases*	=	*Ending Inventory* +	*Cost of Goods Sold*
$0	$120		$30	$90

Table contines on next page.

Table 16.10. Continued

B. Recorded Transactions, Cost of Goods Sold, and Ending Merchandise Inventory

	Operating Cash Flow	*Merchandise Inventory*	*Revenue / Sales*	*Expense / Cost of Goods Sold*
Purchase 1	– 30	+ 30		
Purchase 2	– 90	+ 90		
Sale—Part 1	+ 100		+ 100	
Sale—Part 2		– 90		– 90
Subtotals	**– 20**	**+ 30**	**+ 100**	**– 90**

This method and assumption is referred to as *Last-In, First-Out, abbreviated LIFO.* Notice that the acronym refers to the assumption we are making to determine Cost of Goods Sold. And, once we've determine COGS then we can determine Ending Inventory by subtraction. That is, \$0 + \$120 – \$90 = Ending Inventory.

LIFO implies First-In, Still Here, or FISH. FISH refers to the assumption we are making about Ending Inventory. Once we've determined Ending Inventory we can determine COGS by subtraction. That is, \$0 + \$120 – \$30 = Cost of Goods Sold.

We should make an important point here about our assumptions. In Financial Accounting we can make an assumption about costs independent of what happens in the physical world. We may not even know for certain what happened in the physical world. For example, what if we do not know which physical unit of inventory was actually sold and what unit is still on hand? All we know for certain is that one unit was sold and one unit remains in inventory. We can still make an assumption, like LIFO, for record keeping purposes. This is called a *Cost Flow Assumption.*

The second point to make is that Cost Flow Assumptions are just that, assumptions. For example, some students find the LIFO assumption to be especially odd. Their statement is usually something like, "No business would ever sell the last unit they purchased and keep the first unit they purchased on hand because they would end up with a bunch of obsolete inventory."

Just because we use LIFO for record keeping purposes does not mean we are actually managing our physical units of inventory on a LIFO basis. In fact, The Cost Flow Assumption is completely separate from the physical movement of goods through our inventory system.

Assumption 3: What if we simply averaged the costs in inventory and recorded an average cost for COGS and Ending Inventory? Answer 3: If this assumption is valid then we get the answers in Table 16.11 for COGS and Ending Inventory.

Table 16.11. Average Cost Flow Assumption

A. Units of Currency:

Beginning Inventory +	*Purchases*	=	*Ending Inventory +*	*Cost of Goods Sold*
$0	$120		$60	$60

B. Recorded Transactions, Cost of Goods Sold, and Ending Merchandise Inventory

	Operating Cash Flow	*Merchandise Inventory*	*Revenue / Sales*	*Expense / Cost of Goods Sold*
Purchase 1	– 30	+ 30		
Purchase 2	– 90	+ 90		
Sale—Part 1	+ 100		+ 100	
Sale—Part 2		– 60		– 60
Subtotals	**– 20**	**+ 60**	**+ 100**	**– 60**

This method and assumption is referred to as the *Average Cost* method. Note that with this method it should be obvious that this is an assumption with no connection to the physical world because we did not buy any units for $60, yet we are recording one unit sold at a cost of $60 and one unit retained in Ending Inventory at a cost of $60.

What if we were able to determine the actual, physical unit that was sold? If this were the case, we would not need to make The Cost Flow Assumption. The cost associated with the unit sold would be the amount recorded for COGS and the amount associated with the unit remaining would be our Ending Inventory.

This is referred to as the *Specific Identification* method. It can be, and is, used in some industries. Historically, it was used with items that had low sales volume, but high cost per unit. Otherwise, it was not practical or feasible to go to the effort of tracking costs to specific units sold. As technology continues to advance it is making this method practical in more circumstances.

SUMMARY

Determining the cost associated with COGS and Ending Inventory is part of the broader issue of Deferred Expenses. We buy something today and record an Asset, then consume it or sell it later and the Asset becomes an Expense.

In this chapter we calculated COGS and Ending Inventory using three common Cost Flow Assumptions: FIFO, LIFO and Average Cost. Table 16.12 recaps the results we obtained with these three methods.

Table 16.12. Comparison of Results with FIFO, LIFO, and Average Cost Flow

	FIFO		*LIFO*		*Average Cost*	
Sales		$100		$100		$100
Beg. Inv.	$0		$0		$0	
+ Purchases	120		120		120	
= COGAS	120		120		120	
– End. Inv.	90		30		60	
= COGS		30		90		60
Gross Profit		$70		$10		$40

Note that our measure of profitability, Gross Profit, varies a good bit depending upon the cost flow assumption we use. Gross Profit is the highest with the FIFO assumption, the lowest with the LIFO assumption, and somewhere in between with the Average Cost method.

LIFO is very popular in the United States despite the fact that it often results in a lower reported amount of profit than does FIFO or Average Cost. Why would anyone ever want to report lower profit, when they could make a different, valid, legal, and acceptable assumption to report higher profit? Your hint is what we all have to file each year by April 15th.

CHAPTER 17

OPERATING ACTIVITIES

Inventory, Part II

INTRODUCTION

This chapter continues with the expense transactions associated with operating activities. Chapter 16 introduced the basic concepts associated with inventory cost flow assumptions, a special case of Deferred Expenses. This chapter will provide an additional example of the inventory cost flow assumptions and then conclude with a relatively brief discussion of Accrued Expenses.

INVENTORY COST FLOW ASSUMPTIONS: ANOTHER EXAMPLE

Assume the information in Table 17.1 regarding beginning inventory and purchases:

There are several things to note about the information in Table 17.1. First, the items in boldface text are calculated figures that you should be able to determine yourself. The total cost column is column (2), units, multiplied by column (3), cost per unit. COGAS is the summation of beginning inventory plus purchases. Second, regardless of how

Financial Accounting: A Course for All Majors, pp. 131–137

Table 17.1. Beginning Inventory and Purchases for Chapter 17 Inventory Example

(1)	(2) Units *	(3) Cost / Unit =	(4) Total Cost
Beginning Inventory	2	$10	**$20**
Purchase 1	2	20	**40**
Purchase 2	1	25	**25**
COGAS	**5**		**$85**

information is presented in a problem typically the best thing you can do is organize it in a table like Table 17.1.

Given the information shown in Table 17.1, assume that 3 units of inventory were sold during the period. What is COGS and Ending Inventory under the three inventory cost flow assumptions, FIFO, LIFO, and Average Cost?

If 3 units of inventory were sold then how many units remain in Ending Inventory? We have 5 units available for sale minus 3 units sold equals 2 units in Ending Inventory. This will not change as we alter our cost flow assumption.

> The inventory cost flow assumption affects how many units of currency get allocated to COGS and Ending Inventory, but it has no affect on the number of physical units sold or in ending inventory.

To organize our work, we're going to use the following format shown in Table 17.2:

Table 17.2. Recommended Format to Solve Inventory Cost Flow Assumption Problems

	Units *	Cost / Unit =	Total Cost
Beginning Inventory	2	$10	**$20**
Purchase 1	2	20	**40**
Purchase 2	1	25	**25**
COGAS	**5**		**$85**
Ending Inventory	**2**	?	?
COGS	**3**		**COGAS – Ending Inventory**

In Table 17.2 note that we have arranged The Inventory Equation so that we will be determining Ending Inventory first, then solving for COGS by subtraction (i.e., COGAS – Ending Inventory = COGS). It may not be apparent why this order has been chosen, but from experience we know that for many inventory problems this format will be quite efficient.

The FIFO/LISH Inventory Cost Flow Assumption is shown in Table 17.3:

Table 17.3. FIFO Inventory Cost Flow Assumption

	Units *	*Cost / Unit* =	*Total Cost*
Beginning Inventory	2	$10	**$20**
Purchase 1	2	20	**40**
Purchase 2	1	25	**25**
COGAS	**5**		**$85**
Ending Inventory	**1**	**25**	**25**
	1	**20**	**20**
COGS	**3**		**$40**

We note that the first part of the acronym, FIFO, refers to how we calculate COGS. Since we have chosen to calculate Ending Inventory, we concentrate on the second part of the acronym, LISH – last-in, still-here. The last unit purchased was 1 unit at $25 so we assume it is still in ending inventory. We know there are 2 units in ending inventory so we still have to account for the cost of 1 more unit. Moving up one line on the table we find that the next purchase was 2 units at $20 each. We only need to account for 1 more unit in ending inventory so we record 1 unit at a cost of $20. This gives us an Ending Inventory cost of ($25 + $20) $45. By subtraction, we determine COGS is ($85 – $45) $40.

The LIFO/FISH Inventory Cost Flow Assumption is shown in Table 17.4:

Table 17.4. LIFO Inventory Cost Flow Assumption

	Units *	*Cost / Unit* =	***Total Cost***
Beginning Inventory	2	$10	**$20**
Purchase 1	2	20	**40**
Purchase 2	1	25	**25**
COGAS	**5**		**$85**
Ending Inventory	**2**	**10**	**20**
COGS	**3**		**$65**

Again, we concentrate on the last part of the acronym, FISH – first-in, still-here, and we still need to account for 2 units in Ending Inventory. The first units acquired in this case would be the 2 units that were in

Beginning Inventory, so we record those units and their cost as our Ending Inventory. By subtraction we determine our COGS, $65.

Finally, the Average Cost Inventory Cost Flow Assumption is reported in Table 17.5:

Table 17.5. Average Cost Flow Assumption

	*Units **	*Cost / Unit =*	*Total Cost*
Beginning Inventory	2	$10	**$20**
Purchase 1	2	20	**40**
Purchase 2	1	25	**25**
COGAS	**5**		**$85**
Ending Inventory	**2**	**17**	**34**
COGS	**3**		**$51**

The average cost per unit is $85 / 5 units = $17 per unit. We apply this amount to the two units in Ending Inventory to arrive at a total cost in Ending Inventory of $34. By subtraction, we determine COGS is ($85 – $34) $51.

We summarize our answers in Table 17.6:

Table 17.6. Summary of Inventory Cost Flow Assumptions With Check Figure

	COGS	*Ending Inventory*	*Total*
FIFO	$40	$45	$85
LIFO	65	20	85
Average Cost	51	34	85

Note that a built-in check figure, or reasonableness test, for our answers is that COGS plus Ending Inventory must add up to COGAS. This follows from The Inventory Equation. Checking our work we see that COGS plus Ending Inventory adds up to $85 for all three methods above. This does not guarantee we are correct, but if they did not add up to $85 it would guarantee that we were wrong!

Here is a question that often causes students' eyes to glaze over—which method results in the highest reported profit? Often, students just stare at the results in Table 17.6 and can't get from those figures to an answer to this question. This is unfortunate because we've done the hard work to answer this question by calculating COGS.

Think about the definition, Sales minus COGS = Gross Profit. We do not know what Sales is in this example, nor do we need to know, because regardless of what value Sales is, it will be the same for all three methods;

the inventory cost flow assumption does not change the selling price to the customer. *Since Sales is a constant, what method will maximize Gross Profit? The answer is the method that minimizes COGS.* In this example the correct answer then is FIFO.

What method results in the lowest reported profit? The method that minimizes Gross Profit must be the method that maximizes COGS, LIFO in this example. In times of inflation, or rising prices associated with your purchases, LIFO will always yield the highest COGS and the lowest reported profit. LIFO is popular in the United States because it minimizes reported net income. When used for income tax purposes, LIFO will therefore minimize income taxes.

The Inventory Cost Flow Assumption is one of the rare cases in the U. S. where what is done for income tax purposes is also what must be done for financial accounting purposes. Hence, if a firm wants to use LIFO to minimize their income taxes they must also use LIFO in their financial statements.

INVENTORY ERRORS AND MANIPULATIONS

> What would happen if you thought you had one unit still on the shelf in ending inventory, but when you went to look for it there was nothing there? Where is it? Gone. Perhaps someone stole it, or broke it, and forgot to tell you about it. What adjustment would you need to make on your accounting records? What happens to an Asset when it's used up or no longer has future value? It becomes an Expense, in this case it would probably be recorded as Cost of Goods Sold (or perhaps Cost of Goods Stolen).

This story is intended to highlight the interconnection between what is reported for Ending Inventory and what is reported for COGS. The cost of inventory must be reported one place or the other. If it is still on hand, it should be reported in Ending Inventory, an Asset on The Balance Sheet. If it is gone, then it should be reported in Cost of Goods Sold, an Expense on The Income Statement.

If we think we have one unit in ending inventory, but it's really not there, we have overstated our Ending Inventory. Overstating our Ending Inventory has the opposite affect of understating COGS. One of the things auditors have to be very concerned about is whether firms are accurately reporting their inventory figures. If a firm claims they have inventory that really does not exist, they are overstating their Assets and understating their Expenses. Finally, understating their Expenses will do what to Net Income? It would overstate Net Income.

In one very high profile fraud case a manufacturer of computer hard disk drives actually put bricks in packages and told the auditors the packages contained hard disk drives. Why? The company was claiming more Ending Inventory than they actually had on hand. By overstating their Ending Inventory they were understating their Expenses and overstating their Net Income to make their company appear more profitable. Now, when the auditors came to verify the company's claim about inventory, the company needed to have some "evidence" to substantiate the claim. Their evidence was the packages containing bricks. The company's scheme rested upon their hope that the auditors would not open the packages containing bricks, thereby discovering the fraud. In a large warehouse with thousands of packages, finding the bricks could be like looking for a needle in a haystack. This example points out how devious people can be when misstating their financial results and how difficult an auditor's job can be to detect it.

ACCRUED EXPENSES

A company will encounter a variety of accrued expenses as they incur expenses before they pay the related bill. Examples include payroll costs when the end of an accounting period does not coincide with a regular pay date and routine accounts payable with vendors who provide us with goods or services and allow us to pay at a later date.

There are other, less obvious, accrued expenses. For example, what if a firm sells a product with a one year guarantee? The Matching Principle states that if we are going to record the revenue from the sale then we also need to record all the measurable, anticipated costs of the sale. In this case the firm would need to record an estimate of the cost of honoring the guarantee. This would be recorded in exactly the same manner as any other accrued expense—increase Liabilities and decrease Equity by recording an Expense. This example differs from accounts payable or payroll in that the amount is less certain since it is an estimate of future returns and the future is always uncertain.

Another common example of an accrued expense relates to interest on borrowed money. Since borrowing money is one of the ways we finance our business, we will cover this topic in Chapter 19 when we begin our discussion of financing activities.

SUMMARY

This chapter concludes our discussion of the expense transactions associated with the operating activities of a firm. Chapters 16 and 17 have concentrated on the difficult issue of Deferred Expenses in general, and inventory cost flow assumptions in particular. These assumptions (LIFO, FIFO, and Average Cost) can be a bit deceptive; students often feel like they have the material mastered, or that it is "easy," but then find themselves missing questions they are certain were correct. We state this to reassure you that this is fairly common and to encourage you to persevere.

CHAPTER 18

INVESTING ACTIVITIES

Long-Term Assets and Cost Allocation

INTRODUCTION

Chapters 13–17 covered some key aspects related to the operating activities of a firm. We will not turn to the investing and financing activities. This chapter focuses on investing activities and Chapters 19, 20, and 21 covers financing activities.

INVESTING TRANSACTIONS

In the context of this course, investing transactions refer to the process of acquiring long-term assets, where long-term is defined as something that could reasonably be expected to have value or provide benefits for more than 1 year. This discussion is couched in terms of investing activities for a business organization. Investing activities for an individual typically involve deciding how and where to allocate the money we have set aside for future purposes like retirement or college savings accounts. The personal investing decisions will have to wait for another class as we will be quite busy covering the basic investing transactions for a business.

Financial Accounting: A Course for All Majors, pp. 139–145

A BRIEF OVERVIEW OF LONG-TERM ASSETS

The following is a brief outline of the long-term assets to be discussed in this chapter:

1. PP&E, Tangible Assets, or Fixed Assets
    - (a) Land
    - (b) Buildings, Furniture, Equipment, Machinery, Vehicles, etc.
    - (c) Natural Resources
2. Intangible Assets
    - (a) Externally Acquired
    - (b) Internally Developed
        - i. Advertising
        - ii. Research & Development

ACQUISITION

The initial decision to acquire a long-term asset is complicated, but essentially involves a comparison of costs today with anticipated benefits in the future. In the context of financial accounting, the cost today is the investing cash outflow to buy the asset; the anticipated benefit in the future is the revenues we can generate from using this asset in our business. *The basic entry to record the purchase of a long-term asset is to decrease Investing Cash Flow and increase the related Asset.* The cost of a long-term asset includes all the costs associated with acquiring the asset and getting it ready for its intended use, including transportation and installation. When we record the cost of an item as an Asset rather than an Expense, we say we have *capitalized* its cost.

One might ask why you would exchange something as valuable as cash for something with uncertain future value like land, buildings, equipment, or machinery. The answer lies in what we hope to gain from the asset versus what we can earn from merely investing the cash in, say, a savings account. We might be able to earn 5% on a savings account. In contrast, perhaps we anticipate that a collection of assets devoted to a commercial construction business could earn a 20% return. It might make some intuitive sense, then, to exchange cash for construction equipment even though there is substantial uncertainty involved in running a construction business.

THE MATCHING PRINCIPLE AND COST ALLOCATION

The Matching Principles states that we should record the cost of earning revenues in the same time period as the related revenues. This is quite a challenge with long-term assets because you are potentially making a large investing cash outflow immediately with the anticipation of earning revenue from that asset for several years in the future. If the revenue will be recognized over the future life of the asset, The Matching Principle dictates that we also recognize the cost of the asset as an Expense over the life of the asset too. In financial accounting, this process is referred to as Cost Allocation.

> Cost allocation is the process of recognizing the cost of a long-term Asset as an Expense over its useful life so that we are matching the cost of the Asset with the Revenues derived from the use of the Asset.

We use different terms for Cost Allocation depending upon the asset it is related to, as reflected in the Table 18.1:

Table 18.1. Cost Allocation Terminology

Asset	*Cost Allocation Term*
Land	Not Subject to Cost Allocation
Natural Resources	Depletion
Other Tangible Assets	Depreciation
Intangible Assets	Amortization

Although the terms, depletion, depreciation, and amortization differ, in this context they all mean Cost Allocation.

Why isn't Land subject to Cost Allocation? The rationale is that Land has an unlimited useful life. If you go back to the definition of Cost Allocation it states we are allocating the cost of an Asset *over its useful life*. If an Asset has an unlimited useful life then an argument can be made that we should not allocate its cost. This is the argument we make in financial accounting with Land.

COST ALLOCATION: BASIC EXAMPLE

Assume we are going to buy an Asset, say, equipment that will cost us \$500, will have a three-year useful life, and will be worth \$50 at the end of three years. During the asset's 3-year useful life, we expect the asset will allow us to earn revenues of \$200 per year. Table 18.2 shows how we would use the Cost Allocation process to follow The Matching Principle:

Table 18.2. Cost Allocation and the Matching Principle

	Year 1	*Year 2*	*Year 3*	*Total Yrs. 1-3*
Revenue	$200	$200	$200	$600
Depreciation Expense	150	150	150	450
Difference	$50	$50	$50	$150

Since we were referring to equipment in the example above, we used the term Depreciation in the table above. If we were referring to a natural resource, like oil or natural gas, then we would call this Depletion. Likewise, if the asset were an intangible asset, such as a Copyright, Patent, or License, then we'd call it Amortization. Regardless of what term we use, or what asset it refers to, the basic process of cost allocation is an attempt to match the cost of a long-term asset with the revenues it helps generate during its useful life.

DEFINITIONS

Table 18.3 contains many of the key definitions for the remainder of this chapter. Study it carefully now.

Table 18.3. Some Important Cost Allocation Terms and Definitions

Term	*Definition*	*Example*
Cost, or Historical Cost	The cost of the long-term asset.	Equipment cost = $500.
Salvage, or Residual, Value	The estimated worth of the asset at the end of its useful life to us.	Equipment estimated to be worth $50 at the end of three years.
Depreciable Cost	Cost minus Salvage Value.	$500 – $50 = $450.
Depreciation Expense	Periodic portion of the depreciable cost charged to expense.	$150 per year, calculated as ($500 – $50 / 3 years).
Accumulated Depreciation	The *cumulative* portion of the depreciable cost that has been charged to expense.	This is *time dependent.* At the end of year 1, $150, end of year 2, $300, and end of year 3, $450.
Book Value	Cost minus Accumulated Depreciation.	This is *time dependent.* At the end of year 1, $350, end of year 2, $200, and end of year 3, $50.

The terms Accumulated Depreciation and Book Value can be difficult so we will show in Table 18.4 how we are getting these values:

Table 18.4. Accumulated Depreciation and Book Value

	Year 1	*Year 2*	*Year 3*
Cost	$500	$500	$500
– Accumulated Depreciation	150	300	450
= Book Value	$350	$200	$50

We should note that Accumulated Depreciation is an accumulation of the amount charged to Depreciation Expense each year. At the end of year 1 it is the year 1 Depreciation Expense; at the end of year 2 is the year 1 plus the year 2 Depreciation Expense; at the end of year 3 it is the year 1 plus year 2 plus year 3 Depreciation Expense.

The asset's Book Value is an accounting definition, no more, no less. It is the cost of the asset minus its accumulated depreciation. Importantly, the asset may be "worth" more or less than its Book Value. The cost allocation process is a prediction about the future because it involves an estimate of the asset's life and an estimate of what the asset will be worth at the end of its useful life. Unless those estimates are perfect, the asset's true market value will differ from its reported Book Value.

When the asset is sold if it brings more than book value, we say we have experienced a "gain"; if it brings less than book value we have experienced a "loss." This is summarized in Table 18.5.

Table 18.5. Gain or Loss on Sale of Depreciable Assets

Sale Proceeds > Book Value	Gain
Sale Proceeds = Book Value	Neither
Sale Proceeds < Book Value	Loss

For example, what if we sold the equipment at the end of year 3 for $75? We would have a $25 gain because the sale proceeds of $75 exceed the equipment's book value of $50. What if instead we sold the equipment to a scrap metal dealer and only got $5? We would then have a loss of $45.

STRAIGHT-LINE COST ALLOCATION

There are several mathematical ways to allocate cost. The approach used in the example above is the most common and is called the Straight-Line Method. Besides being easy to calculate it does a nice job of following The

Matching Principle if it is reasonable to conclude that the asset will generate about the same amount of revenues each year during its useful life.

Annual Straight-Line Cost Allocation = (Cost minus Salvage Value) / Useful Life, Years

THE BOOKKEEPING PROCESS

The entry to record the periodic cost allocation always reduces Assets and reduces Equity. We are arguing that we are using this asset up a bit at a time and what always happens to an asset when it is used up? The Asset becomes an Expense.

In the case of cost allocation we typically use a contra-account to record this entry. That is, rather than reduce the Asset account directly, we create a contra-asset account called Accumulated Depreciation. Like all contra accounts, it reduces the related account.

With this qualification, we should restate the entry to record cost allocation. *It would reduce Assets with an entry to a contra-asset account and it would reduce Equity with an entry to an Expense account.*

INTANGIBLE ASSETS

Externally Acquired intangible assets are those that we buy from another in an exchange transaction. If a company buys a Patent, then its cost is whatever they paid the seller for it, and they follow the cost allocation procedures discussed above.

Internally Developed intangible assets are another story. These are assets that we create ourselves, rather than buying them from an outside party. Let's go through a few examples to make this more concrete.

- Example 1 is a company that spends a great deal of money on advertising and promotion to create brand awareness for its product. A notable example would be Coke. What is the intangible asset? We could call it Brand Awareness. How much would it be worth?
- Example 2 is a company that has a research lab and develops a patent on a new process to convert switch grass to ethanol. Since this is reportedly a much cheaper process than using corn, this patent could have tremendous value. What amount should we record for the patent?

- Example 3 is a company that has an excellent reputation for customer service. Nordstrom might be a good example here. How much is this asset, call it Reputation, worth?

These are the types of situations we're dealing with in the area of internally developed intangible assets. Often, there is not much argument that an Asset exists, but objectively *measuring* the value of the Asset can be quite difficult. As a compromise, we use the following general rule with internally developed intangible assets in the United States:

For internally developed intangible assets we only record as an Asset the cost of acquiring the legal rights to the associated intangible asset. All other costs associated with developing the intangible asset are recorded as an Expense when they are incurred.

For example, in the case of an internally developed Patent we would have to hire a patent attorney to file the paperwork to document our idea and secure our legal protection with the government. The cost of securing this claim is recorded as an Asset, but the cost of actually coming up with the idea is recorded as an Expense.

The general rule leads to the following with respect to two key areas. *The costs associated with Advertising and Research & Development are expensed as incurred.* Again, the argument in accounting is not so much whether an asset is being created, but rather how to put an amount on its value. We follow the principle of *conservatism* in this area by requiring everyone to simply expense these costs, rather than allowing them to record amounts that could be inflated.

SUMMARY

This chapter concludes our coverage of investing activities and cost allocation. Chapters 19–21 will cover financing activities which include borrowing money from others (i.e., debt) and obtaining money from owners (i.e., equity).

CHAPTER 19

FINANCING ACTIVITIES

Simple Interest and Amortized Loans

INTRODUCTION

This chapter will begin a discussion of the financing type activities of an organization. Recall that the two primary ways to finance an organization are debt (i.e., borrowed money) and equity (i.e., owners' money). This chapter will concentrate on debt financing, Chapter 20 will address a topic called the time value of money, and Chapter 21 will cover equity financing topics.

IS DEBT GOOD OR BAD?

Debt can be a controversial subject. Debt, or borrowed money, can be a good thing and a bad thing. At a personal level, debt is good because it allows us to buy things today and pay for them tomorrow. Perhaps the most common use of debt at the personal level is to buy a house or a car, relatively expensive items. Few of us could afford to pay cash for either, so the ability to borrow the money for these items *improves our standard of living*. In a business context, many business ventures that have greatly

Financial Accounting: A Course for All Majors, pp. 147–156

advanced the welfare of society would never have gotten off the ground had the business not been able to borrow some money to get started. If used responsibly, debt is not a "bad" thing.

Debt is a bad thing when it is used irresponsibly. We will classify the problems we see with debt at the personal level into two categories. *The first problem is borrowing more than you can repay given a reasonable estimate of your current and projected income level at the time of the borrowing.* Debt is borrowed money and borrowed money is supposed to be repaid. This sounds simple, but too many people conveniently ignore this reality; the short-term pleasure then leads to long-term pain when the bills come due.

Note that we have qualified the statement above by saying "at the time of the borrowing." There is an old saying that bad things happen to good people. The problem we are highlighting here is when people borrow more than they can repay given their circumstances at the time they borrowed the money. It is another thing entirely to have a subsequent event (e.g., medical disability) cause financial problems. We have no magic answer for financial problems that are caused when bad things happen to people who have otherwise been responsible with their finances.

The second problem is related to the first but we will state it separately. It is common to finance a house with a 30-year loan. Why does this make sense, but financing a laptop computer with a 30-year loan does not make sense? In corporate finance we have a basic tenant that states you should *match the maturity of the debt with the life of the asset being financed.* At a personal level, many people violate this principle by financing things with little, if any, long-term value using lengthy loans. When the loan term exceeds the useful life of the asset this leads to the problem of "owing more than the asset is worth".

BASIC BORROWING TRANSACTIONS

When an individual or company borrows money the basic transaction is to increase Financing Cash Flow and increase Liabilities. When this money is later repaid the reverse is true—Financing Cash Flow and Liabilities are both reduced.

THE CONCEPT OF INTEREST

Interest is what the lender charges the borrower for the use of their money. Most of us have probably paid rent for an apartment or house. Rent is the price we pay for the temporary use of the landlord's asset. Likewise, interest is the price we pay for the temporary use of the lender's money. Just as rent is considered an Expense, *interest is also reported as an Expense on The Income Statement.*

The starting point to calculate interest is the formula for *Simple Interest* shown in Table 19.1:

Table 19.1. Simple Interest Formula

Principal (P) *	Rate (R) *	Time (T)
Amount Borrowed	Periodic Interest Rate	Number of Periods

In the formula above, it is important that the Rate and Time elements be consistent. For example, *the interest rate is generally on an annual basis unless explicitly stated otherwise; that is the practice we will follow in this course.* Consequently, if the interest rate is expressed on an annual basis, then the time element must also be in annual units.

Example 1: Assume you borrow $5,000 at 10% interest for 1 year. How much interest will you owe on this loan? $5,000 * .10 * 1 = $500. Note here that since that since we're using an annual interest rate we could omit the time element and by default have the correct answer for 1 year since multiplication by 1 does not change the answer.

Example 2: Assume you borrow $5,000 at 10% interest for 2 years. How much interest will you owe on this loan? $5,000 * .10 * 2 = $1,000.

Example 3: Assume you borrow $5,000 at 10% interest for 9 months. How much interest will you owe on this loan? $5,000 * .10 * 9/12 = $375. Note here that the interest rate is for 1 year but the term of the loan is only for a portion of a year, 9 months. Therefore, our time element must be for the proper *fraction of a year,* 9/12ths.

Example 4: This example will combine the concepts of interest and accrual basis accounting. On July 1, 20X1, assume you borrow $5,000 at 10% interest for 9 months. The loan plus all of the interest will be due and payable on March 31, 20X2. How much interest should be recorded as an expense in 20X1? 20X2?

The total amount of interest on this loan will be $5,000 * .10 * 9/12 = $375. What portion of this total falls in 20X1? July 1 through December 31, or 6 months, pertains to calendar year 20X1 so how much Interest Expense should be recorded in 20X1? There are two ways to answer this question. We prefer the first, but we'll report both and leave it to the reader to decide which option is best for them.

- $5,000 * .10 * 6/12 = $250 Interest Expense for 20X1.
- $5,000 * .10 * 9/12 = $375 total Interest Expense for 20X1 and 20X2. Since 6 of the 9 months occur in 20X1, then $375 * 6/9 = $250 Interest Expense for 20X1.

*In the illustration above, here is what you do not want to do: $5,000 * .10 * 6/9 = WRONG ANSWER!*

If the total interest from July 1, 20X1, to March 31, 20X2, is $375, and $250 pertains to 20X1 then the remainder, $375 – $250 = $125, must be Interest Expense for 20X2. Using the accrual basis of accounting we are allocating the total Interest Expense between the two accounting periods, 20X1 and 20X2, since these are the two accounting periods that benefited from the use of the borrowed money.

Here is a diagram similar to the one used in Chapter 9 when we covered adjustments:

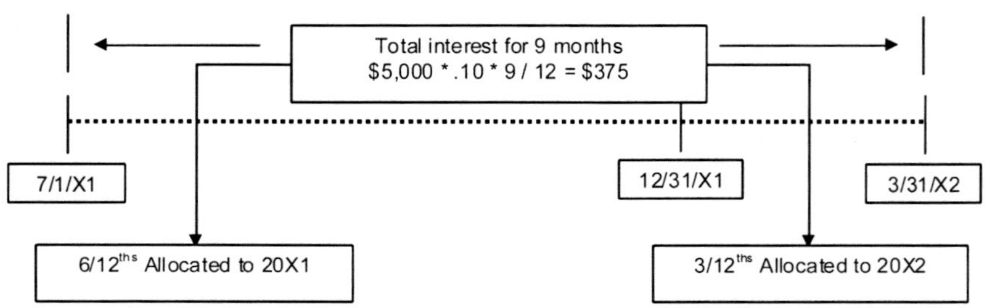

Figure 19.1. Allocation of Interest Expense Between Two Periods.

Table 19.2 shows how this borrowing transaction will be recorded. We are going to show the borrowing and repayment of the principal first:

Table 19.2. Borrowing and Repayment of Principal

	Financing Cash Flow	*Note Payable*
July 1, 20X1 Borrowing	+ 5,000	+ 5,000
March 31, 20X2 Repayment	– 5,000	– 5,000

As we stated earlier, the initial borrowing increases Financing Cash Flow and Liabilities (Notes Payable); the repayment does the opposite.

The interest expense component would be reported as follows:

Table 19.3. Allocation and Payment of Interest Expense

	Operating Cash Flow	*Interest Payable*	*Interest Expense*
July 1, 20X1			
December 31, 20X1		+ 250	– 250
March 31, 20X2	– 375	– 250	– 125

We have intentionally included a line for July 1, 20X1, in Table 19.3 because students often want to record a liability for interest at the inception of the loan. With Simple Interest, interest accrues day-by-day so we do not have a liability for interest at the inception of the loan. Rather, it accrues over time and it is just a matter of convenience that we choose to only record it at year-end on December 31st and the maturity of the loan, March 31st.

We should also note that *the payment of interest, unlike the receipt and repayment of the loan principal, is reported as an Operating Cash Flow.* For the sake of brevity, we will not try to explain the rationale for this practice.

AN AMORTIZED LOAN

Many loans require that we make frequent, periodic payments instead of lump sum payments at the maturity of the loan. Most of us probably have a car or house loan like this. In these cases, a portion of each payment pays for interest and the remainder goes toward reducing the principal.

Let's assume that you borrow $1,000 at 10% for 4 years with 4, equal payments of $315.47 required to repay the loan plus interest. How much of each payment is interest and how much is principal? To answer this question, let's use an *Amortization Table* like the one in Table 19.4 (next page). You should pause here and spend some time working through Table 19.4. Here are some things to note about an amortized loan:

- The interest component of each payment, Column (4), gradually declines over time. This should make some intuitive sense because Column (4) is a constant percentage of Column (2), which is gradually decreasing over time.
- The payment is constant, so as the interest component declines over time the portion of each payment going to reduce the loan balance (i.e., principal) increases.
- The required, periodic payment of $315.47 "amortizes," or pays off, the loan plus interest by the end of the loan term. This is shown in the Amortization Table on the last line, Column (10) where the Ending Balance is zero. *We will learn how to calculate the amount of the periodic payment in the next chapter.*

FINANCIAL LEVERAGE

We'll continue this chapter with a powerful concept related to debt financing. From physics we borrow the term leverage, meaning to magnify or enhance a given amount of energy.

Table 19.4. Amortization Table

(1)	*(2)*	*(3)*	*(4)*	*(5)*	*(6)*	*(7)*	*(8)*	*(9)*	*(10)*
Period	*Beginning Balance*	+	*Interest*	=	*Subtotal*	–	*Payment*	=	*Ending Balance*
1	$1,000.00		$100.00		$1,100.00		$315.47		$784.53
2	$784.53		$78.45		$862.98		$315.47		$547.51
3	$547.51		$54.75		$602.26		$315.47		$286.79
4	$286.79		$28.68		$315.47		$315.47		$ –

Column (2) Starts at $1,000 and then is from Column (10) one period earlier in subsequent periods.

Column (4) = Column (2) * .10 (because the interest rate is 10%).

Column (6) = Column (2) + Column (4).

Column (10) = Column (6) – Column (8).

Let's assume you have the opportunity to buy an asset for $10,000 and this asset will provide you with $1,000 of income per year for as far as the eye can see. We'll assume you only have $5,000 of your own money (i.e., equity) available so you'll have to borrow $5,000 if you want to buy this asset. Let's assume you can borrow money from a rich aunt at an interest rate of only 5% per year. What rate of return will you earn on this investment?

Let's recap first. You have invested $5,000 of your own money and in exchange acquired an asset that will generate $1,000 of income each year. Since you borrowed $5,000 at 5% interest you owe your rich aunt $250 per year interest, or rent for the use of her money.

Your annual income from this investment is $1,000 – $250 = $750. On a percentage, or rate of return basis, you are earning $750 on your investment of $5,000, which is a ($750 / $5,000) 15% return on your investment. The asset itself is only earning ($1,000 / $10,000) a 10% rate of return so how can you earn 15%? The answer lies in the fact that you have used debt to your advantage. You borrowed money from your rich aunt at 5%, invested it in an asset earning 10%, and you get to keep the excess return. In corporate finance, we call this *financial leverage and it occurs whenever you can invest borrowed funds in assets that will earn more than the cost of the borrowed money.*

Unfortunately, financial leverage cuts both ways. What if the asset above was expected to produce $1,000 of income per year but in reality it only generates, say, $300 per year in income. You still owe your rich aunt $250 per year rent on her money so your annual income is $300 – $250 = $50 on your investment of $5,000, which is only a ($50 / $5,000) 1% rate of return. In this case, your rate of return, 1%, is less than the asset's rate of return, 3%, because you financed part of the asset with debt having an interest rate that exceeded the return on the asset.

Financial leverage is positive when you invest borrowed money to earn a return higher than the cost of the debt; financial leverage is negative when you invest borrowed money to earn a return lower than the cost of the debt.

BONDS: A FANCY IOU

Government entities and larger companies have the ability to borrow money from "the market," meaning the collection of people like you and I (except with more money!) who have money to lend if the terms are mutually agreeable. This is often referred to as "issuing bonds," or "selling bonds." A bond is just a synonym for a corporate IOU.

Visualize a bond as a piece of paper, the IOU, which spells out the terms of a borrowing and lending agreement. It could be as simple as the following:

IOU \$1,050, One Year from Today

How much would you give me for the piece of paper, the bond, pictured above? (Not to digress, but the paper itself isn't worth anything, but the legal claim that it represents is what might have value if you can trust me to repay you.)

If you give this much thought at all, you'll eventually conclude that *the amount you'd be willing to loan me today in exchange for \$1,050, one year from today depends upon the interest rate you want to earn on this loan.* For example, if you were willing to make me an interest-free loan, then you could loan me \$1,050 today and you'd get your money back 1 year from now.

Assume you wanted to charge me, say, 5% interest. How much would you loan me today? Let X be the amount today and solve the following: X + .05X = \$1,050. In this case, X = \$1,000. So, if you loan me \$1,000 today and get \$1,050 back in one year you would have earned your desired 5% interest rate.

Let's draw up a fancier bond with some new terms on it in Figure 19.2.

Face Value = \$1,000
Stated Interest Rate = 5%
Maturity Date = One Year from Today

Figure 19.2. Example Bond.

The *Face Value is the single, lump sum amount to be repaid on the Maturity Date.* It corresponds to the Principal in our earlier examples with loans. The Stated Interest Rate means that the owner of this bond is entitled to receive *5% of the Face Value (\$1,000 * .05) \$50 per year interest.* The Maturity Date is when the bond is paid off, or retired.

You should note that the two IOUs above are equivalent in the sense that both promise the owner, or holder, of the bond \$1,050 one year from today. The second bond simply divides that total into two parts, \$1,000 Face Value and \$50 Stated Interest.

What would happen if you changed your mind and only wanted to loan me money if you could earn 20% interest? This is possible and we don't even have to change the terms of the bond above. Let X again be the amount you'd be willing to loan me and solve for the following: X + .20X = \$1,050. In this case X = \$875. This means that if you give me \$875 today in exchange for my promise to pay you $1,000 "Face Value" plus $50 "Stated Interest", a total of $1,050, then you will earn your desired 20% interest rate.

In Table 19.5 we summarize how much we've determined this bond would be worth under three different scenarios:

Table 19.5. Inverse Relationship Between Market Rates and Bond Prices

Lender's Desired Interest Rate	*Bond Price*	*Terminology*
0%	$1,050	Premium
5%	1,000	Face Value
20%	875	Discount

We can make some observations, or generalizations, about bonds from this table.

- If the lender's desired interest rate increases, the value of a bond decreases, and vice versa.
- If a bond is selling for *more than Face Value* we say it is selling at a *Premium.*
- If a bond is selling for *less than Face Value* we say it is selling at a *Discount.*
- If, and only if, the lender's desired interest rate is exactly equal to the Stated Interest Rate will the bond will be worth its Face Value.

Why do bonds not always sell at face value? Typically, the issuer of a bond would like the bond to sell near face value so they will try to set the stated interest rate to be equal to the lender's desired rate of return. However, they do not know for certain what the lender's required rate of return will be when the bonds are actually sold because there is a time lag of several weeks between setting the stated interest rate and selling the bonds. The bond certificates have to be printed and the issuer has to comply with legal and regulatory requirements before they can sell the bonds to the public. This delay means that by the time the bonds are issued to the public, the people buying the bonds may want a higher, or lower, rate of return than what is printed on the bond certificates. As we have seen, they can easily accomplish this by adjusting the price they are willing to pay for the bond.

Furthermore, someone who buys a bond today may later decide to sell it to someone else tomorrow. As time passes, circumstances change and the lender's desired interest rate may increase or decrease. Rather than tear up the bond and start fresh, we keep the same bond but adjust the price that a lender agrees to pay for it. As we've seen above, if you don't like the stated interest rate on a bond it is a relatively easy matter to get a different rate of return by changing the price you are willing to pay for the bond.

An easy way to remember this important relationship between the market rate of interest and the selling price of a bond, is to envision a teeter totter. When one side (market rates of interest) goes up, the other side (selling price of the bond) goes down. This is illustrated in Figure 19.3.

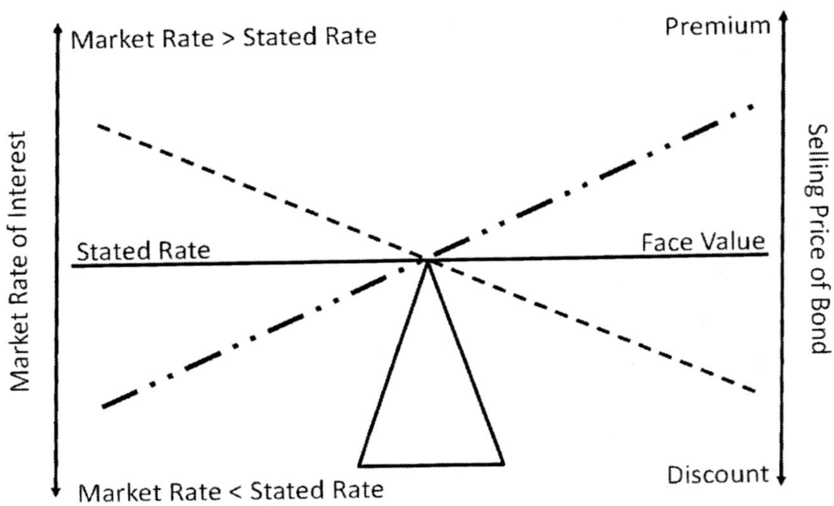

Figure 19.3. Teeter Totter Illustration of Corporate Bond Price and Market Rates of Interest.

SUMMARY

This chapter introduced the concepts of simple interest, amortized loans, financial leverage, and bond pricing. The next chapter will cover the Time Value of Money, which is a very useful topic for everyone when making financial decisions.

CHAPTER 20

FINANCING ACTIVITIES

The Time Value of Money

INTRODUCTION

Some courses in Financial Accounting may omit this topic. We have omitted it in our own courses as our attitudes have changed over the years. Business majors are required to take Business Finance and will learn similar material in that course. Nonbusiness majors will not, however, so this might be the only exposure they will ever get to this extremely useful topic.

THE TIME VALUE OF MONEY

One of the most powerful tools in personal and corporate finance is referred to as the time value of money. In short, it means that a dollar received today is not worth the same amount as a dollar to be received in, say, 10 years. The dollar received today is worth more because you could invest it for 10 years and earn interest.

The mathematics of the time value of money are important, but they are not our concern in this book. Rather, we are going to focus on learning how to utilize the financial functions built into the Excel spreadsheet

Financial Accounting: A Course for All Majors, pp. 157–169

so that you might be able to answer some very practical time value of money problems in your personal or professional lives.

First, we will define some terms and provide the abbreviations used in Excel. These appear in Table 20.1. To access any function in Excel, just click on the function button, *fx*, that should appear on the line immediately above the worksheet.

Table 20.1. Time Value of Money Definitions and Abbreviations

Term	*Abbreviation*	*Description*
Present Value	PV	An amount to be given or received today, at time zero.
Future Value	FV	An amount to be given or received at some point in the future.
Interest Rate	Rate	The periodic interest rate that is assumed. Note that Rate is often expressed on an annual basis, but Rate can be for another unit of time; the most important point to remember is that Rate and Nper must always be expressed in consistent units.
Number of Periods	Nper	The number of periods of time in the application. Note that the unit of time for Nper is often one year, but Nper can be another unit of time (e.g., month).
Amount of Payments	PMT	The dollar amount of each payment in a series of equal, periodic cash flows. For example, car loans are usually repaid in equal, monthly amounts over the term of the loan. PMT is the monthly amount, not the grand total of all payments combined.
Annuity		A series of equal, periodic cash flows.

EXAMPLE 1: FV FUNCTION

Assume you invested $2,000 into a savings account when you were 25. How much would you have 40 years later when you were 65, assuming the investment earned 8% interest? We'll use the Excel function, FV, to answer this question since we're going to be calculating a Future Value. This is shown in Figure 20.1.

In the screen shot, note that the interest rate is entered as a decimal equivalent, .08, rather than as a percentage. Also note that the PV was entered as a negative number since this would be an outflow to us today when we deposit the money into the savings account. The "formula result" is the answer to our question. Or, if you click OK the answer will be entered in the worksheet. In this case the FV will be $43,449.

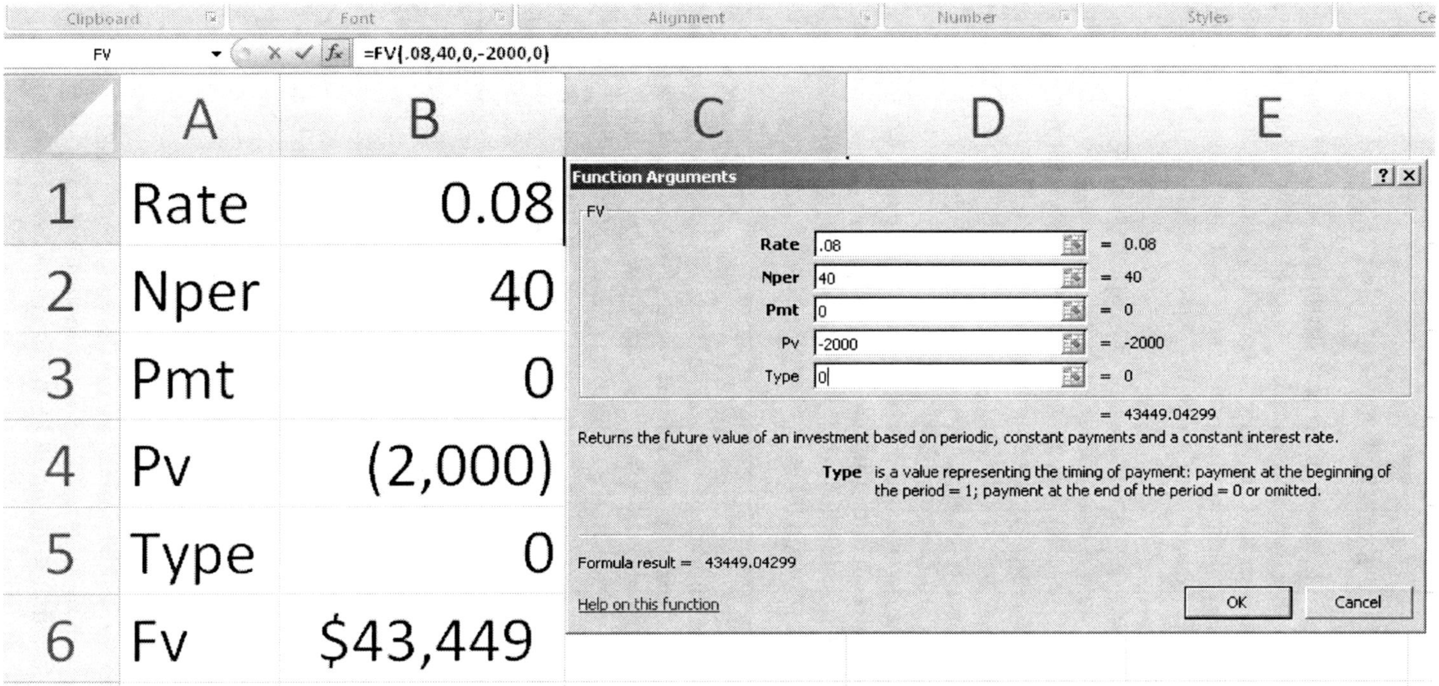

Figure 20.1. Illustration of the Future Value (FV) Function in Excel.

EXAMPLE 2: RATE FUNCTION

Let's assume again that you will invest $2,000 into a savings account when you are 25, but this time you want it to grow to $50,000 by the time you are 65. What interest rate would you have to earn to attain this goal? In this case we're searching for an interest rate that would make $2,000 grow to $50,000 in 40 years so we'll use the RATE function. This is shown in Figure 20.2.

As you can see, the formula result is 8.38% (rounded). It may be hard to believe that such a minor change in the interest rate could have that much difference but it's true. Keep in mind that this "minor increase" in the interest rate is having a compound effect over 40 years. The bottom line for this investor is that an increase of only 0.38% results in the account being worth $6,551 more (in percentage terms this would be a [$6,551 /$43,449] 15% increase!).

This example also illustrates why good financial advisors urge their clients to seek investments with low annual costs. Lower costs increase returns to the investor and relatively small changes can accumulate to large amounts over long periods of time.

Please note in the screenshot (Figure 20.2) that the PV was entered as a negative number and the FV was entered as a positive number. The idea is that the PV represents an outflow, or negative amount, for you today as you put this money aside into the savings account. When you withdraw this money in 40 years the FV will be an inflow, or positive amount. It is rather arbitrary which one is positive and which one is negative, but they need to be opposite in sign for the Excel function to work properly.

EXAMPLE 3: NPER FUNCTION

Let's continue with our assumption that we will invest $2,000 into a savings account when we are 25. In this example let's assume that the best return we can attain is 8%. If we can't change the interest rate, let's see how many more periods we would have to let this investment grow to equal $50,000. We'll use the Excel Nper function to answer this question, which is illustrated in Figure 20.3.

You can see this if we can just let the investment grow for 41.82 years, rather than 40, we can accomplish our goal. If we still want the money when we're 65 then we need to invest the money about 2 years earlier. If we can't start until we're 25, we'll need to let the money grow until we're about 67. Note that the PV and FV had to once again have opposite signs to solve this problem.

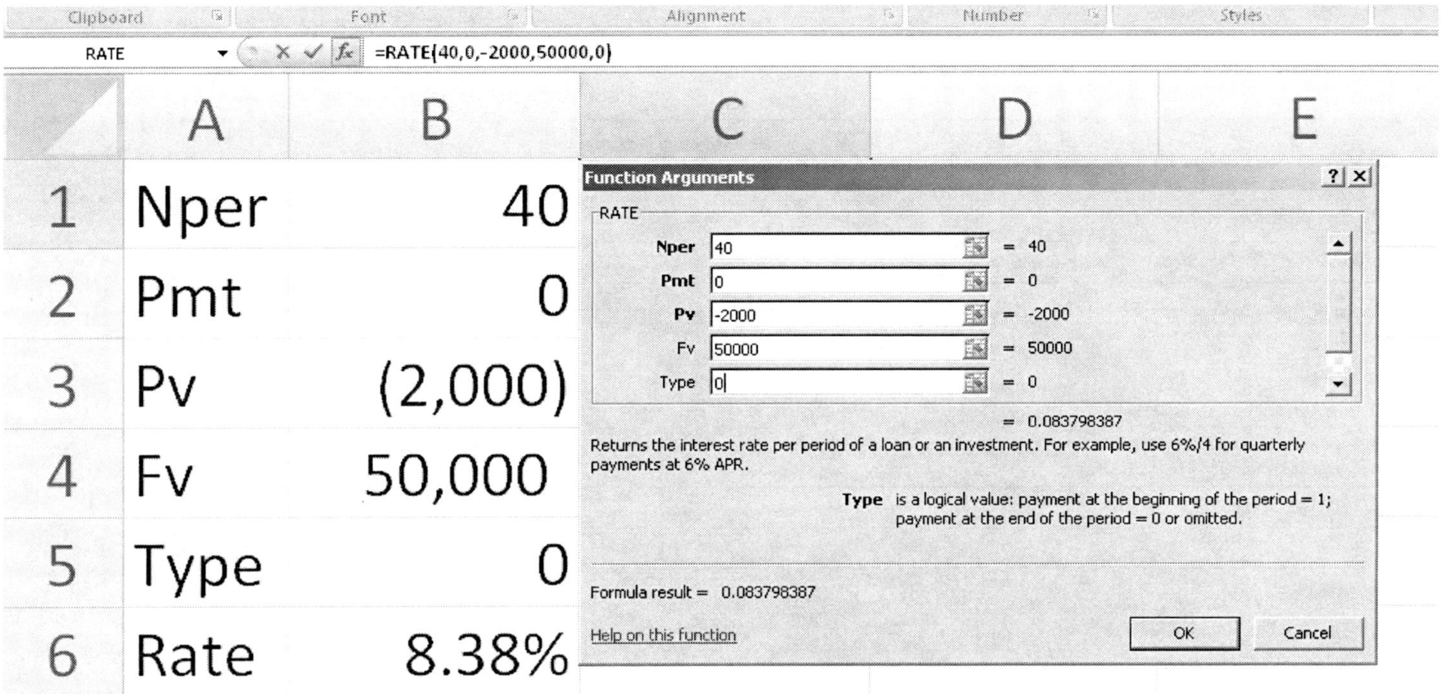

Figure 20.2. Illustration of the Rate Function in Excel.

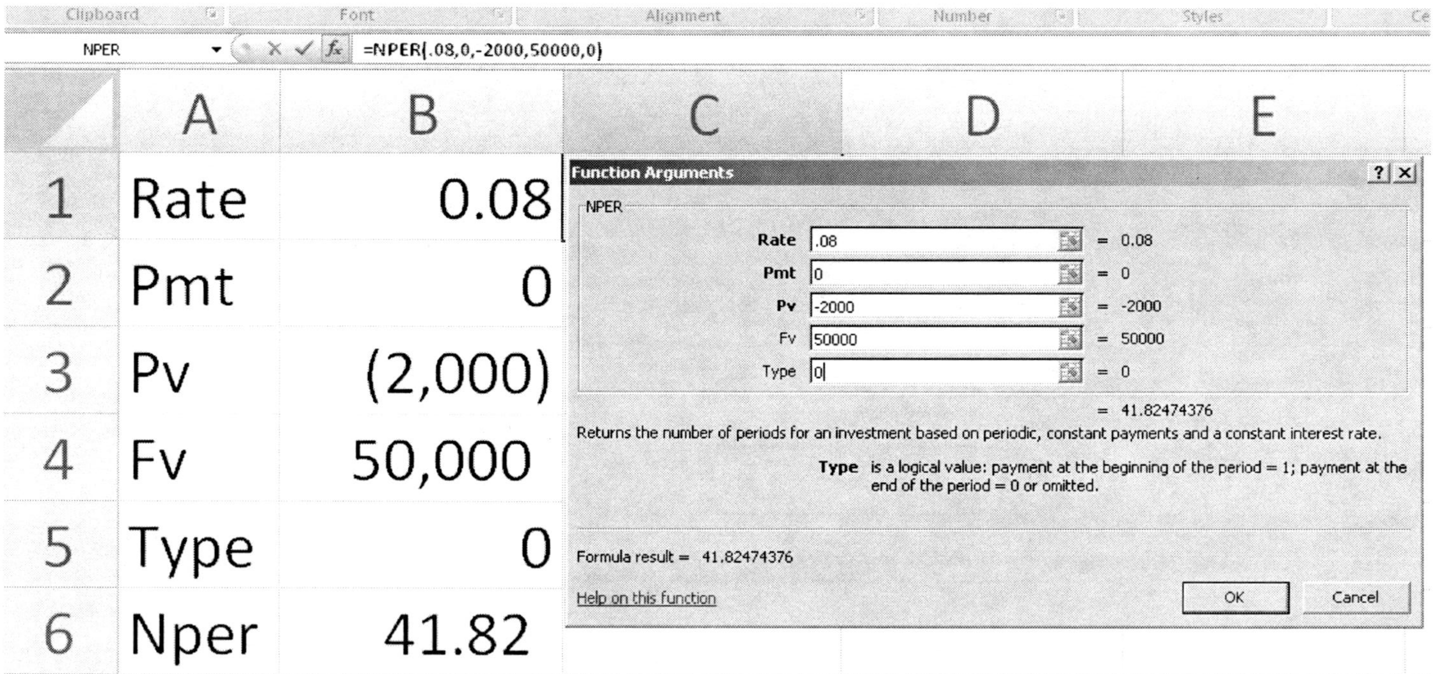

Figure 20.3. Illustration of Number of Periods (Nper) Function in Excel

EXAMPLE 4: PV FUNCTION

Let's consider a completely different example. If you'd like to have $1,000,000 accumulated by the time you're 65, how much would you have to invest when you're 25 to accomplish this goal? Assume the interest rate is 8%. This is an example of the Excel PV function and is illustrated in Figure 20.4.

So, if you could invest $46,031 (rounded) when you're 25 it would grow to $1 million when you're 65. That's not a bad deal, but most people could not come up with that much money to invest at one time, especially not when they are so young.

EXAMPLE 5: PMT FUNCTION

Let's tweak our problem in Example 4 above to be a bit more reasonable. That is, how much would we have to save *each month* for 40 years to accumulate $1,000,000 for retirement? The Excel PMT function answers this question as shown in Figure 20.5. This answer, $286.45 per month, may surprise you. This is the power of compound interest and the time value of money that an investment of (only) $286.45 per month earning interest at 8% for 40 years grows to $1 million.

In the screenshot note two very important adjustments that had to be made to answer this question. Since we were assuming monthly payments, we had to change the Nper to (40 years * 12 months per year) 480. The interest rate of 8% is per year; in time value of money calculations you always need to express Nper and Rate in consistent terms. That is, if one is expressed in months then the other must be expressed in months. To express Rate in months, we simply wrote .08 / 12 above.

EXAMPLE 6: ANOTHER APPLICATION OF THE PMT FUNCTION

A common use of the PMT function is to determine what one's monthly payments would be on a car or home loan. We can't tell you how many times over the years that we have been asked to calculate payments for our friends. You're going to see that it is an easy task for anyone to do on their own.

Let's assume you'd like to buy a home for $100,000. Typically, you would need to come up with some initial cash, called the down payment. If your down payment was $5,000, you will need to borrow $95,000. What would your monthly payment be on a $95,000 home loan at 6% interest and paid off over 30 years? Figure 20.6 shows that this is a relatively easy problem to solve using Excel's PMT function.

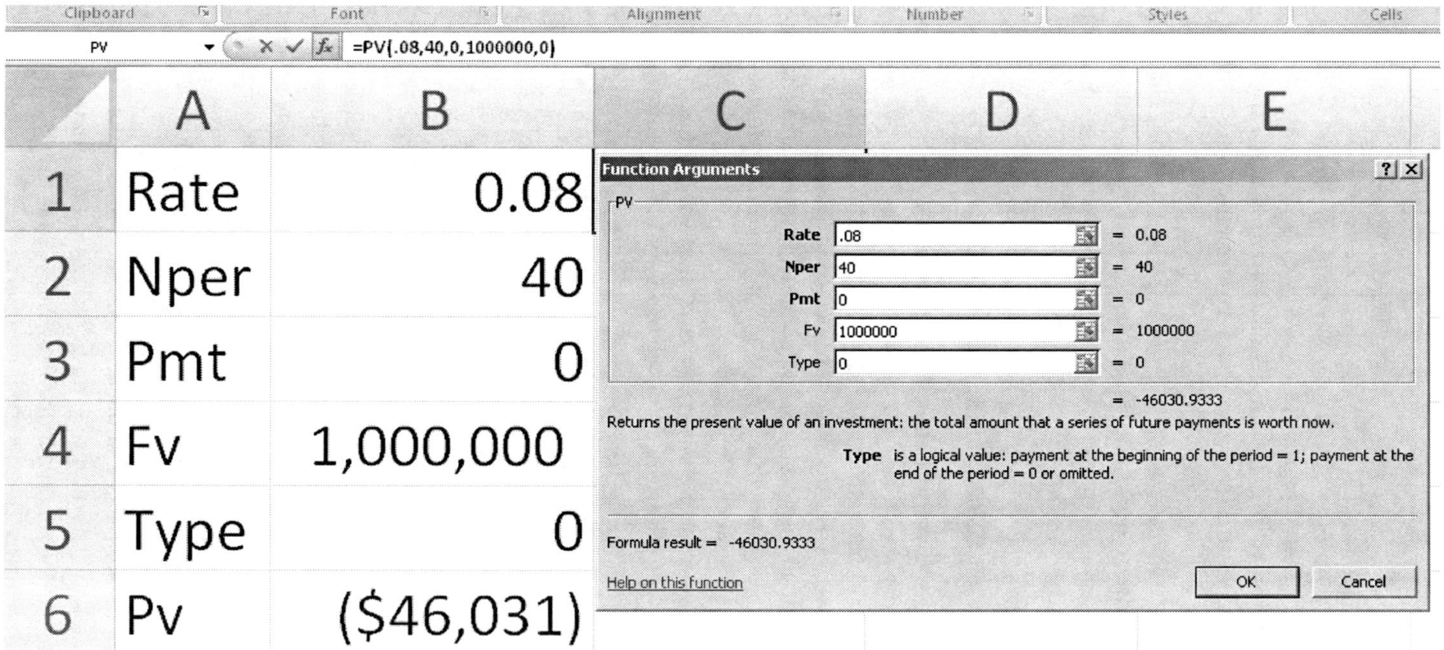

Figure 20.4. Illustration of Present Value (PV) Function in Excel.

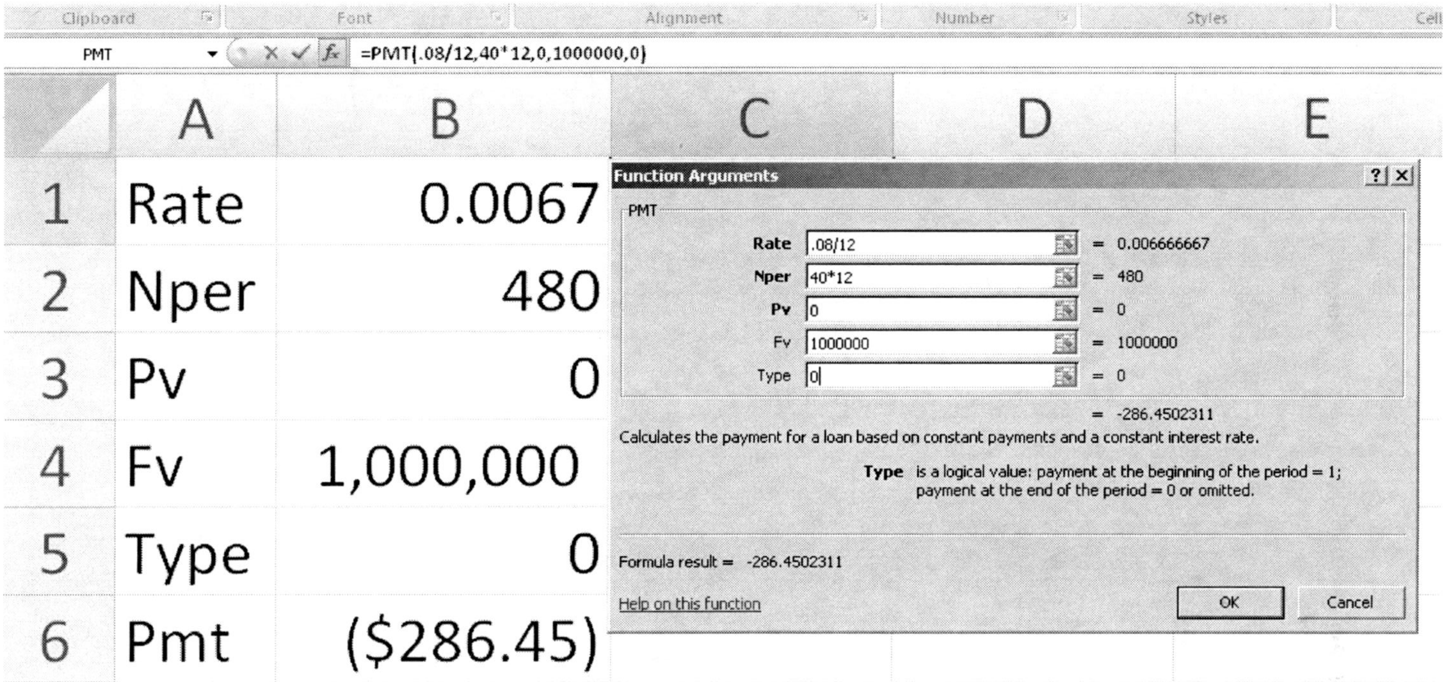

Figure 20.5. Illustration of the Payment (PMT) Function in Excel.

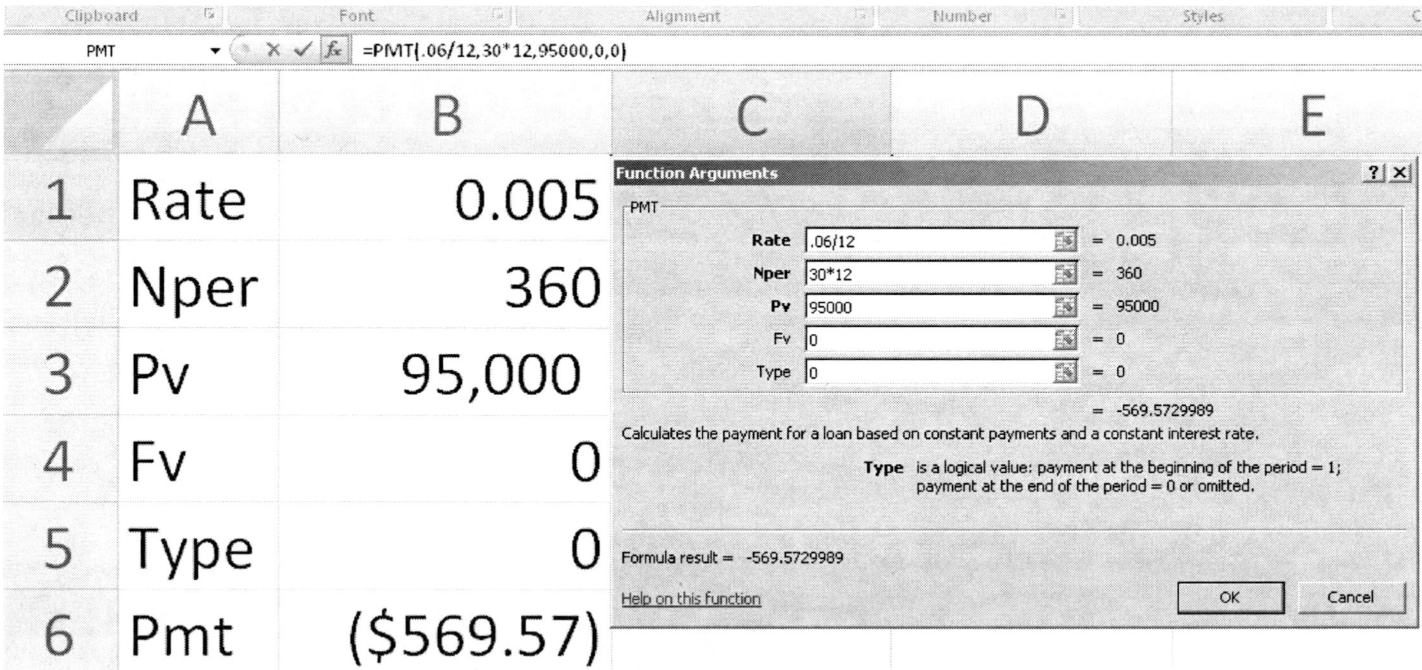

Figure 20.6. Illustration of the Payment (PMT) Function in Excel.

Your monthly payment will be $569.57. Note that the PV above is $95,000, the amount you would need to borrow today to finance the purchase of your home. The FV is set to zero to show that you must have the loan paid off at the end of 30 years. It also seems like we should repeat that Nper is 30*12 since we want to calculate a monthly payment and the Rate is .06/12 for the same reason.

FINDING THE SELLING PRICE OF A BOND

As we learned in Chapter 19, certain corporations or governments can borrow by issuing IOUs called bonds. A bond typically has a face, or par, value of $1,000, meaning it will repay the owner of the bond $1,000 at maturity. The bond will also have a stated interest rate, which is the *percent of the face value* that will be paid each period as interest.

Let's assume a bond has a face value of $1,000, a stated interest rate of 5%, and a maturity date that is 15 years from now. The bond pays interest annually. Please note the future value (FV) is the single amount the owner of the bond will receive at maturity, $1,000. The payment (PMT) is the periodic amount the owner will receive each period as interest, or rent, on their invested funds. In this case it is (5% * $1,000 face value) $50. The number of periods (Nper) is 15, since the bond matures in 15 years.

The difficult concept with bonds is that the amount you would be willing to pay for the bond today, the present value (PV), depends on the interest rate that you want to earn on the investment. And, the interest rate you want to earn on the investment is completely independent from the stated rate of interest on the bond. Let's assume you want to earn 8% on this bond. How much would you be willing to pay for the bond today? This is a present value question that can easily be answered with the PV function as shown in Figure 20.7.

The answer is $743.22 (rounded). Note that since the bond is only paying a stated rate of 5% and you want to earn an amount greater than that, 8%, you must pay less than face value, less than $1,000, in order to earn your required rate of return. When a bond is acquired at less than face value we say the bond is selling for a *discount*. You might recall the teeter totter illustration from Chapter 19 which was used to visualize the inverse relationship between market rates of interest and the selling price of a bond. We invite you to prove that if you were willing to accept a rate of return that was less than 5% then the bond would sell for more than $1,000, which is called a *premium*.

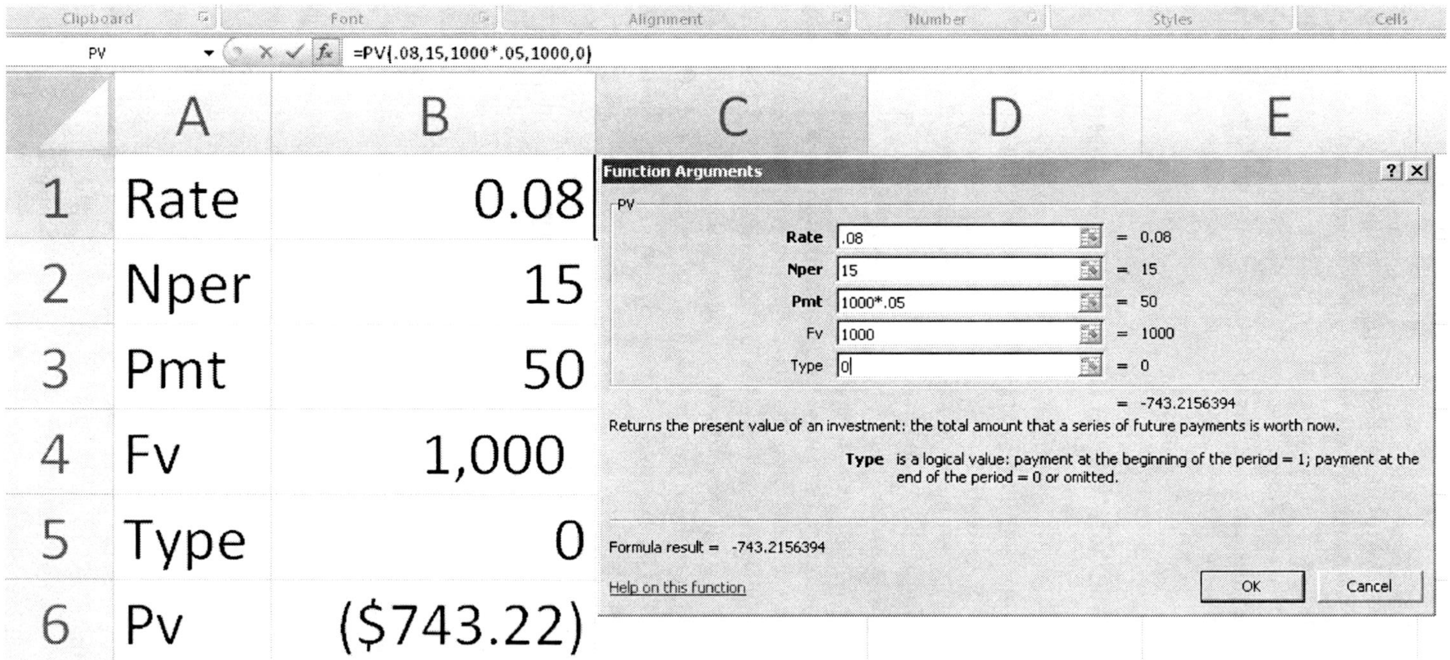

Figure 20.7. Illustration of Using the Present Value (PV) Function in Excel to Determine the Selling Price of a Bond.

SUMMARY

We believe the tools illustrated in this chapter can be incredibly useful to you throughout your life as you plan for financial events such as accumulating a down payment for a house, saving for retirement, investing for college, or determining whether you can afford the payments on a new toy. Although it is tempting to simply remain ignorant about the time value of money and let others do the work for you, we are talking about your money and no one will care as much about your money as you do. Spend half as much time learning to manage your money as most people do planning how they will spend it and you will be on the road to financial stability.

CHAPTER 21

FINANCING ACTIVITIES

Equity Transactions

INTRODUCTION

This chapter concludes our discussion of the financing type activities of an organization. Recall that the two primary ways to finance an organization are debt (i.e., borrowed money) and equity (i.e., owners' money). This chapter will concentrate on some issues surrounding equity financing.

THE CHOICE OF BUSINESS ENTITY

Although this class includes a variety of majors from all fields, business majors do not have a monopoly on starting businesses. You may be the next person to start their own business so we'll provide a bit of background here on one of the important choices you'll need to make. One of the first choices to be made when starting a business is deciding upon the type of entity to be used. There are several choices and several considerations as listed in Table 21.1 (next page).

Financial Accounting: A Course for All Majors, pp. 171–179

Table 21.1. Considerations in the Choice of a Business Entity

Type of Entity	*Limited Liability*	*Double Taxation*	*No. of Owners*
Sole Proprietorship	No	No	1
General Partnership	No	No	2 or More; Limited
LLC	Yes	No	1 or More; Limited
Corporation—"S Corp"	Yes	No	1 or More; Limited
Corporation—"C Corp"	Yes	Yes	1 or More; Unlimited

We list five choices under Type of Entity. A Sole Proprietorship is simply an individual deciding to start a business. No new entity is created and the person simply operates under her own name, or she can use a business name by filing a "doing business as" or DBA certificate at the local courthouse. A General Partnership is similar but involves two or more people getting together to start a business. If you get involved in any form of partnership have an attorney document the understanding among all the partners with respect to sharing profits and losses, what happens if one partner dies or withdraws, etc. This can save a lot of heartache and hard feelings later!

The third choice of entity is a Limited Liability Company (LLC). This is a separately created legal entity that functions much like a Sole Proprietorship or General Partnership except it provides for Limited Liability. Limited Liability means the business entity is separate and distinct from its owners so that if a claim is made against the business the owners' personal assets are generally protected. Limited Liability is the reason why many businesses do not operate as a Sole Proprietorship or General Partnership. In such a litigious society, doing so is simply too risky!

The fourth choice is a specific type of corporation, an "S Corp." A corporation is also a separate legal entity that affords its owners liability protection. The S Corp and the LLC appear identical in the table above; in fact, they are quite similar and a qualified tax advisor would be best suited to help make the choice between the two.

The last choice is what most people mean when they say "corporation". A "C Corp" has Limited Liability like an LLC and S Corp but it also has the added advantage of being able to have an unlimited number of owners. This is important for large, publicly traded corporations so that they can attract capital from many potential owners. Regardless of how a business starts, if a business prospers and desires to become quite large it usually has to convert to a C Corp so that it can sell shares of stock to the general public.

Limited Liability of a corporation generally means that the most you can lose is what you have invested in the corporation. The corporation's creditors cannot pursue you personally for any debts of the corporation.

An important caveat to this statement is if the owners have voluntarily relinquished this right. For example, it is common for banks to require small business owners to sign a "personal guarantee" for the debts of a corporation. If the owners choose to sign a personal guarantee, the corporate entity does not shield the owners' personal asset from the bank's claims.

The primary disadvantage of a C Corp is termed Double Taxation. This means that the income of the entity is taxed once at the entity level and then again when those profits are distributed to the shareholders as dividends. When we were discussing a multiple-step income statement in Chapter 12 we included a line for Income Tax Expense because we envisioned the entity being a C Corp and subject to a corporate income tax.

We'll conclude this brief discussion with a caveat. We have not provided enough information for you to make a choice of business entity should you decide to start a business. However, we hope we have provided enough information to make you aware of the importance of this choice so that you will seek counsel from your CPA or attorney.

CORPORATE FORM OF ENTITY

The corporate form of ownership became popular when organizations began to grow larger and it was apparent that they needed to be able to attract money from many individuals. This also led to what is called the *separation of ownership and management.* The traditional corporation is organized as shown in Figure 21.1.

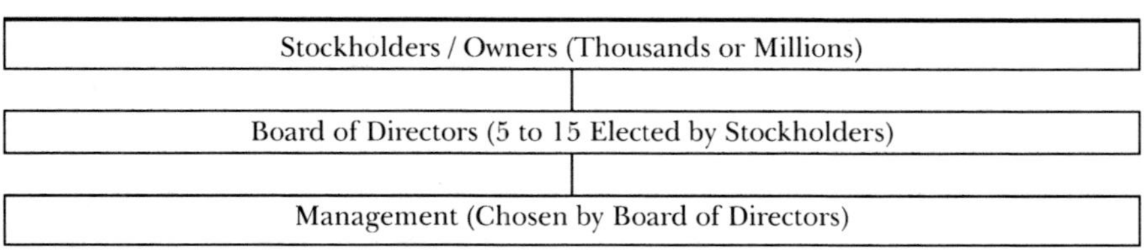

Figure 21.1. Corporate Separation of Ownership and Management.

The owners elect a smaller group, often 5 to 15, called the Board of Directors. The Board's job is to make major policy decisions and to hire Management to run the day-to-day business.

In the corporate form of entity, elections are typically based upon the concept of *one share, one vote.* Therefore, *the person or persons who own the majority of the shares of the corporation are said to have "control,"* meaning they have enough votes to elect their own directors and thereby "call the shots."

Another caveat might be useful here. If you contemplate getting involved in a business and you will be a minority shareholder, meaning others can out vote you on important matters, you might want to approach this situation very carefully. Etiquette and good manners are often replaced by greed and guile as the controlling shareholders take advantage of the minority shareholders.

In addition to the right to vote, we will note two additional stockholder rights. First, stockholders have the right to receive their proportionate share of dividends if and only if the Board of Directors votes to pay a dividend (more on this later). Second, stockholders have the right to receive their proportionate share of funds if the corporation is ever dissolved. This would typically involve converting all the assets to cash, paying all the liabilities and then distributing the remaining cash, if any, to the shareholders in proportion to the number of shares of stock they own.

CORPORATE STOCK

Table 21.2 defines three terms with respect to the ownership shares of the corporate entity.

Table 21.2. Corporate Stock Terminology

Term	*Explanation*
No. of Shares Authorized	How many shares of stock a corporation *may sell* to the public.
No. of Shares Issued	How many shares of stock a corporation *has sold* to the public.
No. of Shared Outstanding	How many shares of stock a corporation still has outstanding, meaning still *owned by shareholders.*

The difference between Issued and Outstanding shares may not be apparent. Assume a company is Authorized by the state in which they incorporated to sell up to 500,000 shares of stock. However, they have only sold 100,000 shares of stock. This leaves them with plenty of room to grow by issuing more new stock (up to 400,000 additional shares) in the future without having to file any additional paperwork with the state. Now, it turns out one of the owners who bought 2,000 shares of the 100,000 shares sold is a perpetual kicker (an old slang term for complainer).

The other shareholders finally decide life would be easier without her so they vote to have the corporation buy her shares back. *Shares that have been sold, but then repurchased by the corporation and are therefore no longer outstanding are called Treasury Stock.* The cost of Treasury Stock is recorded in a *Contra-Equity account*. It is important to note that *Treasury Stock is not an Asset;* an entity can not "own itself."

In our example the number of shares authorized was 500,000, the number of shares issued was 100,000, the number of shares outstanding was 98,000, and the difference between issued and outstanding is 2,000 shares of Treasury Stock.

TYPES OF STOCK

There are two general classes of stock, common and preferred stock. Common stock is what most people refer to when they talk about ownership in a company. Preferred implies preferences, and sure enough the owners of Preferred Stock do get some special treatment. Specifically, *Preferred stockholders get a Dividend Preference and a Liquidation Preference. In exchange for these preferences, Preferred stockholders give up their right to vote in corporate elections. They also typically give up their right to share in all of the company's profits.*

Here is an example to illustrate the Dividend Preference. Assume a corporation has 50 shares of preferred stock with a $100 par value and a 5% dividend rate and additional shares of common stock outstanding (it does not matter how many for this example). The Board of Directors has voted to distribute $600 in dividends. How much will the Preferred shareholders receive? Common shareholders? The answers appear in Table 21.3.

Table 21.3. Allocation of Dividends Between Preferred and Common Stockholders

Total Dividends	$600
Less: Portion to Preferred = $100 * .05 * 50	250
Equals: Balance to Common	$350

Note that the 5% dividend rate means the Preferred shareholders are entitled to receive 5% of $100 before the Common shareholders get anything. However, once the Preferred shareholders get their 5%, then the remainder belongs to the Common shareholders. This leads us to the statement that *Preferred stock is less risky than Common stock, but Common stock has more upside potential for gain than does Preferred stock.*

What if the company above was only going to pay out $200 in dividends? How much would the Preferred shareholders receive? In this case, they would get it all and the Common shareholders would get none.

DIVIDEND PAYMENT PROCESS

Dividends are not an obligation of a corporation until such time as the corporation's Board of Directors votes to pay a dividend. Doing so is called "declaring" a dividend. Once the Board has declared a dividend then it becomes a liability for the corporation. Figure 21.2 illustrates the dividend payment process.

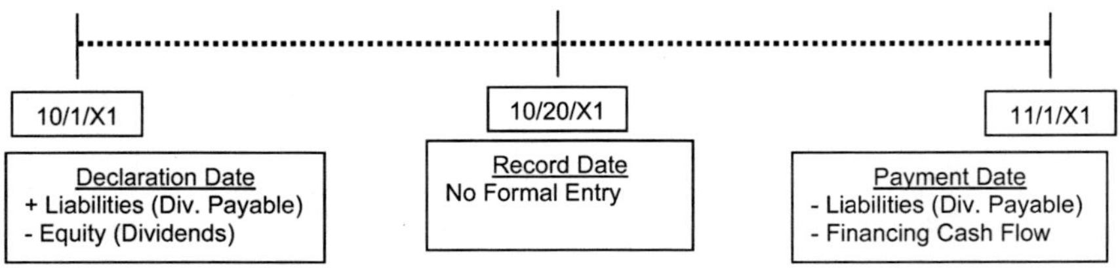

Figure 21.2. Corporate Dividend Payment Process.

In this case the corporation's Board declared a dividend on October 1, 20X1. This increases the corporation's Liabilities (Dividends Payable) because they now have a legal obligation to pay this dividend. This also reduces Equity (Dividends) because it establishes their intent to pay out corporate funds to the shareholders in the near future.

When the Board declares a dividend they also specify a Record Date and a Payment Date. The Record Date determines who will receive the dividends. In this case anyone who owns shares on October 20, 20X1, will receive the dividend; if you buy the stock on October 21 or after you will not receive the dividend. There is not formal entry in the company's accounting records on this date, but someone will have to document the names and addresses of all owners so that checks can be distributed later.

Finally, the Payment Date follows several weeks later on November 1, 20X1. On this date dividend checks are mailed out to all owners of record on October 20. On the Payment Date the corporation is satisfying its obligation to pay the dividend so it will reduce Liabilities (Dividends Payable) and reduce Financing Cash Flow.

SOME BASIC STOCK TRANSACTIONS

The basic entry for a corporation to record the sale of stock is to increase Equity (Contributed Capital) and increase Financing Cash Flow. Some stock has a "par value," which does not have a great deal of practical significance but does change the bookkeeping ever so slightly. Assume a corporation issues 10,000 shares of common stock. Each share of common stock has a par value of $0.01 (one penny) but sells for $50 per share. This would be recorded as shown in Table 21.4.

Table 21.4. Recording the Issuance of Par Value Stock

	Contributed Capital	
Financing Cash Flow	*Common Stock*	*Additional Paid-In Capital*
+ 500,000	+ 100	+ 499,900

The Common Stock is increased for the amount of the par value only, 10,000 shares times $0.01, and the Additional Paid-in Capital is increased for the remainder of $500,000 minus $100 equals $499,900. Note that Contributed Capital still encompasses the entire $500,000 of proceeds from the sale of stock so our basic entry is still to increase Equity (Contributed Capital) and increase Financing Cash Flow. The par value is just a bit of bookkeeping necessity.

If this corporation later bought back 1,000 shares at a cost of $60 per share then they would record the transactions as shown in Table 21.5.

Table 21.5. Reacquisition of Treasury Stock

	Contributed Capital		
Financing Cash Flow	*Common Stock*	*Additional Paid-in Capital*	*Treasury Stock*
+ 500,000	+ 100	+ 499,900	
– 60,000			– 60,000

The reacquisition of stock previously issued decreases Financing Cash Flow and decreases Equity (Treasury Stock). Recall, Treasury Stock is a Contra-Equity account.

STOCK SPLITS

Our final topic in this chapter is stock splits. A stock split involves changing the number of shares of stock in a company holding everything else constant. Let's think about an analogy here. Visualize a pie cut into, say, four pieces. One of the four pieces of the pie has been designated yours so we can say that you own (1/4) one-fourth of the pie. Now, assume that someone decides to cut each of the four pieces in half so that we now have eight pieces of pie. Your one piece is now two pieces so you still own (2/8) one-fourth of the pie. Are you any better off with two pieces than one?

A stock split is similar except we might, under certain assumptions, be somehow able to argue that you are better off with two pieces rather than one. For the most part, though, it just seems like we are cutting the pie (i.e., corporation) into more pieces (i.e., shares).

An X-for-Y stock split means the number of shares will change by X / Y and the value of each share should change by about Y / X.

Assume a company has 10,000 shares of stock with a $1 par value and currently sells for $75. If it undergoes a 3-for-1 stock split, how many shares of stock will it have after the split? How much will the par value of each share be? How much would you expect each share to be worth after the split? We'll summarize our answers in Table 21.6.

Table 21.6. 3-for-1 Stock Split

	Before	*3-for-1 Split*	*After*
Number of Shares	10,000	* (3/1) =	30,000
Par Value	$1	* (1/3) =	$0.3334
Market Value	$75	* (1/3) =	$25**

** Estimated. The market will ultimately decide whether the stock is worth more than, equal to, or less than $25 after the stock split.

In this case we can state with certainty that we will have three times as many shares after the split as before and each share's par value will be one-third of its previous value. We can predict that the market value of the stock will fall by one-third, to $25.

Why do firms engage in stock splits? Corporate finance people feel that there is an optimal price range for a share of stock. We've heard it stated as being in the $20 to $80 per share price range. If a company's share price exceeds, say, $80 it is thought to be detrimental to attracting new investors. The best example here is a company called Berkshire Hathaway whose shares sell for more than $100,000 each. Even if I only wanted to buy one share, you'll have to trust me that I cannot afford it. So, they have excluded me from their list of potential shareholders. Most firms want to attract as many investors as possible so they strive for stock prices in the optimal range. A stock split is one way to keep the price in this range.

There is probably also a psychological appeal to stock splits. Do we somehow feel better with two pieces of pie rather than one piece even if the two pieces are exactly half of the one piece? It reminds us of a story attributed to Yogi Berra. When ordering a pizza he was asked if he wanted it cut into six pieces or eight and he replied, "Better make it eight. I'm pretty hungry." Stock splits might have the same appeal to some people.

Or, what if management's decision to split the stock is a signal that the company is going to prosper in the future? That is, the stock split is a signal that the corporate pie is actually going to get larger. If we believe this, then we would expect our two pieces to soon be larger than the original piece and we will truly be better off. This is the type of thought process that makes it difficult to predict with certainty what the price of a stock will be after a stock split.

SUMMARY

This chapter concludes a three part series on the primary transactions involved in the financing type activities of a company. We've discussed the different forms of a business organization and some of the primary issues surrounding stock and stock ownership. We invite you to stick around for a few more chapters so that we can conclude this textbook and your first course in Financial Accounting.

CHAPTER 22

AN INTRODUCTION TO FINANCIAL STATEMENT ANALYSIS

INTRODUCTION

Thus far in this course we have concentrated our efforts on the process of converting inputs (i.e., transactions) into outputs (i.e., three, major financial statements). Let's put this behind us and assume that the financial statements are complete. What do you do with financial statements? *The process of using financial statements to make decisions is often referred to as Financial Statement Analysis (FSA).* This chapter is an introduction to FSA.

THE CREDIBILITY OF FINANCIAL STATEMENTS

Before we begin the "number crunching" part of FSA, we want to stress what we will refer to as the credibility of the financial statements. Financial statements are only as credible as the people and processes that created them. We will mention three factors to consider in evaluating the credibility of financial statements:

Financial Accounting: A Course for All Majors, pp. 181–187

- Management. The financial statements are ultimately the responsibility of management. If the management team does not have integrity, why would you trust the financial statements they have produced? We cannot tell you how to evaluate management integrity so instead we will pose a question. In your day-to-day life how do you decide who you can trust and who is not worthy of your trust?
- Auditors. Ideally the financial statements used in FSA should have been audited by an external financial statement auditor. An audit by an independent auditing firm gives the reader of the financial statements another level of assurance that the financial statements are credible. We want to stress, however, that an external financial statement audit does not guarantee the financial statements are correct, but it does increase the likelihood that there are no major errors in them.
- Internal Controls. As part of their audit, the external auditors evaluate not only the end result of the financial accounting process, the three major financial statements, but also the process that created them. Since we do not audit every single transaction, the idea is that if we can trust the process that transforms inputs (i.e., transactions) into outputs (i.e., three, major financial statements) then we will have more confidence that the financial statements are correct. The primary way auditors evaluate this process is by reviewing and testing the internal controls that are present. If the company has good internal controls then, everything else being equal, we can have more confidence that the financial statements are credible.

GENERALLY ACCEPTED ACCOUNTING PRINCIPLES

There is one more thing we should mention before launching into our discussion of FSA. Financial statements are supposed to be prepared according to a prescribed set of rules. Just as we have laws and moral codes that dictate right and wrong in our personal lives, there are rules to follow in preparing financial statements. We have discussed these rules at various stages of the course and they include concepts like the Accrual Basis of Accounting, the Revenue Recognition Principle, and the Matching Principle. Collectively, all of the prescribed rules for financial statements are referred to as Generally Accepted Accounting Principles (GAAP). We pronounce the acronym, GAAP, just like the popular retailer, Gap.

We now define Credible Financial Statements as those that are the result of a process with effective internal controls, prepared by a management team with integrity, and audited by an independent, external financial statement auditor to ensure compliance with GAAP.

HORIZONTAL ANALYSIS

One thing that we can learn from financial statements is how an organization has done over time. Quantifying how a particular line item on the financial statements has changed over time is referred to as Horizontal Analysis, getting its name from the fact that we generally put the information in columns from left-to-right and then conduct the analysis.

Table 22.1 illustrates a horizontal analysis on Wal-Mart's sales for the three fiscal years 2005–2007:

Table 22.1. Horizontal Analysis of Wal-Mart Sales

	2005	*2006*	*2007*
Net Sales (000,000s)	$281,488	$308,945	$344,992
Divide by Base Year 2005	281,488	281,488	281,488
Equals Base Year 2005 Index	1.0000	1.0975	1.2256
Times 100	100	100	100
Equals Base Year 2005 Index as Percent	100.00%	109.75%	122.56%

The general formula for this calculation can be stated as follows:

(Analysis Year / Base Year) =
Base Year Index * 100 = Base Year Index as Percent

We should note that there is nothing magical about the choice of a base year other than it is often the earliest year for which analysis will be done. In our case, we decided to limit our analysis to 2005–2007 and used the earliest year, 2005, as our base year.

The results tell us that Wal-Mart's Net Sales in 2006 were 109.75% of what they were in 2005, or we could say that 2006 Net Sales increased by (109.75% – 100.00%) 9.75% over Net Sales in 2005. Likewise, their 2007 Net Sales were 22.56% greater than their 2005 Net Sales.

Perhaps the more important question is whether this is good or bad? To answer this question you need a frame of reference. If Wal-Mart had established an internal goal that 2006 Net Sales would be 12% greater than 2005 Net Sales then they obviously did not meet their internal target and we can say the results are "bad." Another way to answer this question would be to compare Wal-Mart's results to the average results for all the firms they consider to be their primary competitors. Let's assume that the average Net Sales in 2006 for their competitors was 8.5% greater than 2005 Net Sales. By this comparison Wal-Mart's results are "good" since their increase of 9.75% exceeds the industry average.

Our point is that "good" or "bad" really depends upon your frame of reference or comparison point. At a personal level, let's assume you were hoping for a 5% raise next year. When you get your raise you learn that your pay increased 6% and you're happy because that exceeds your internal goal of 5%. However, within the week you learn through the grapevine that the average raise for all employees in your department was 8%. Now, that same raise of 6% that made you happy several days earlier does not seem so "good." Your new pay level has not changed, but your frame of reference has shifted from 5% to 8%, which means your 6% pay raise now leaves you wondering what you did wrong instead of smiling from ear-to-ear. Likewise for companies, they have internal goals, but they also have to compare their results to how competitors have done and how they have fared given the general condition of the economy.

We'll generalize our discussion of Horizontal Analysis by pointing out that it can be done on any item on the financial statements for two or more years.

VERTICAL ANALYSIS

Another form or FSA is called *Vertical Analysis.* It involves expressing each item on an income statement as a percentage of Net Sales, or each item on a balance sheet as a percentage of Total Assets. Since we are most accustomed to seeing this used on the income statement we will illustrate this method in Table 22.2 using figures adapted from Wal-Mart's fiscal 2007 income statement.

Table 22.2. Vertical Analysis of Wal-Mart Income Statement

	Dollars	*% of Net Sales*
Net Sales	$344,992	100.00%
COGS	264,152	76.57%
Gross Profit	80,840	23.43%
All Other Expenses	69,556	20.16%
Net Income	$11,284	3.27%

The general formula to determine the right-hand column is:

(Income Statement Item / Net Sales) * 100 = % of Net Sales

The Vertical Analysis of Wal-Mart's income statement can viewed as telling the reader what happened to each dollar of Net Sales. Let's examine the right-hand column from the top down. We can see that COGS was 76.57% of Net Sales, which means that Gross Profit is (100.00% – 76.57%) 23.43% of Net Sales. This is equivalent to saying that for each $100.00 of Net Sales, $76.57 was used to pay for the goods sold, while $23.43 remained to help Wal-Mart pay for their other costs of doing plus provide a profit to their shareholders.

We should note that the percentages in the right-hand column are consistent with the same addition and subtraction rules as the related dollar figures in the middle column. For example, Sales minus COGS equals Gross Profit so the 23.43% we see in the right-hand column for Gross Profit can be determined in two ways. One is by direct calculation [($264,152 / $344,992) * 100] while the other uses the percentage column and the definition of Gross Profit (100.00% – 76.57%). The fact that the percentages in Vertical Analysis should follow these rules provides a built in check figure for your calculations. For example, if the COGS was 76.57% but the Gross Profit was 40.00% then we know a mistake has been made on at least one of the two items.

Recall that Gross Profit is not the same as Net Income. Out of Gross Profit Wal-Mart must pay all of the other costs of doing business such as wages and salaries, depreciation on buildings, and corporate income taxes. In this case, all of those other expenses consumed 20.16% of each dollar of Net Sales. This left Wal-Mart with 3.27% of each one dollar of Net Sales as bottom line profit, or Net Income.

We should note that two of the figures above have been introduced earlier. The Gross Profit Margin is the name commonly associated with the 23.43% figure above. The Gross Profit Margin is closely monitored by merchandising businesses because it gives them an idea of the difference between what they paid for items versus the eventual selling price to their customers. This "mark up" is a key measure of effectiveness for any merchandising business.

The Net Profit Margin is the name given to the 3.27% figure above. It reflects, in percentage terms, how much profit the business has earned on its Net Sales. This is also a key measure because lenders and investors will not continue to provide funding to Wal-Mart if they are not profitable.

Students are sometimes surprised to see that Net Profit Margins for many businesses are smaller than they anticipated. Net Profit Margins vary a great deal by industry. The grocery industry, for example, typically has relatively low profit margins while a technology company with a dominant market position like Microsoft typically has a relatively high Net Profit Margin. Across all U.S. businesses, Net Profit Margins tend to fall in the 5 to 8% range depending upon which year is examined.

EVALUATING STRATEGY USING GROSS AND NET PROFIT MARGINS

Consider two retailers, Wal-Mart and Neiman Marcus. As most of us know, Wal-Mart's business strategy is everyday low prices. Low prices should translate into low Gross Profit Margins since Wal-Mart cannot mark up their sticker prices a lot over their cost and still follow their business strategy. Low Gross Profit Margins means that Wal-Mart does not have a lot of each dollar of Net Sales remaining to pay for all of the other costs of doing business. This means that they will have to concentrate on keeping all of those other costs low if they want to have a positive Net Profit Margin. The primary way to keep those other costs low is to minimize the amount of services offered to customers. Wal-Mart's stores are not fancy nor do they pretend to offer a great deal of one-on-one customer service. This is part of Wal-Mart's strategy because they feel their customers will accept lower customer service in exchange for everyday low prices.

In contrast, Neiman Marcus caters to upscale customers who probably don't want to be seen at a discount store like Wal-Mart. Neiman Marcus has fancy stores and its customers expect to be pampered. In exchange for a more luxurious shopping experience, their customers are willing to pay higher prices. In fact, the only way Neiman Marcus can pay for these amenities and still be profitable is by charging higher prices.

When we look at their income statement ratios we would expect this to translate into higher Gross Profit Margins for Neiman Marcus as compared to Wal-Mart. We might also expect Neiman Marcus to have a higher Net Profit Margin than Wal-Mart, but that is a riskier prediction since their higher costs may exceed their higher gross protit margins. Table 22.3 reports the two companies' ratios.

Table 22.3. Evaluating Business Strategy Using Ratios

		Wal-Mart	*Neiman Marcus*
Gross Profit Margin	$\frac{\text{Gross Profit}}{\text{Sales}}$	23.68%	34.53%
(Net) Profit Margin	$\frac{\text{Net Income}}{\text{Sales}}$	3.57%	5.78%

We need to conclude this chapter so we'll keep this short. Our basic point is that a firm's business strategy should be reflected in their financial statements and vice versa. We should be able to learn something about a firm's business strategy by looking at their financial statements. In this case, Neiman Marcus does in fact have a higher Gross Profit Margin than Wal-Mart. In the year we examined, Neiman Marcus also had a higher Net Profit Margin than Wal-Mart.

Does this mean that Wal-Mart is "unsuccessful?" No. It is simply a reflection of the fact that Wal-Mart has made a conscious decision to follow a business strategy that differs from Nieman Marcus. We will see in the next chapter that which firm is most "profitable" really depends upon how you define profitable.

SUMMARY

This chapter introduced you to the concept of Financial Statement Analysis (FSA), which we have defined as the process of using financial statements to make decisions. We have also stressed that useful FSA must be performed on credible financial statements. Effective analysis on faulty financial statements is worthless. The next chapter will conclude our brief introduction to FSA.

CHAPTER 23

FINANCIAL STATEMENT ANALYSIS AND RATIO ANALYSIS

INTRODUCTION

The previous chapter introduced the topic of Financial Statement Analysis (FSA) including horizontal and vertical analysis. This chapter will concentrate on the subtopic of FSA called ratio analysis.

RATIO ANALYSIS

Ratio analysis simply means relating one thing (i.e., numerator) to another thing (i.e., denominator). In previous chapters we have already done a bit of ratio analysis without giving it a formal name. For example, the Gross Profit Margin and the Net Profit Margin are both ratios. This chapter will introduce some additional ratios commonly used in corporate FSA.

Before we get too far into this topic, we want to note that ratio analysis is much broader than simply memorizing the several ratios presented in this chapter. Ratios certainly appear in situations other than a Financial

Financial Accounting: A Course for All Majors, pp. 189–198

Accounting class. Consider the following examples of ratios in other contexts:

- Baseball fans love statistics and many of those statistics are ratios. Measures like batting average (the ratio of hits to at bats) or earned run average (the ratio of earned runs times innings in a game divided by innings pitched) are key ratios in a baseball context.
- In healthcare, most hospitals monitor their bed utilization ratio (number of beds occupied divided by total bed available) very closely as it is a key measure of capacity utilization.
- During the restructuring of the U.S. automotive industry we have been hearing a good bit about General Motors and Chrysler shutting many of their local dealerships. Dig a bit deeper and you will find a ratio—the ratio of vehicles sold per year divided by the number of dealerships. This ratio is a measure of the efficiency of the dealer network. Toyota has a very efficient dealer network (i.e., a higher ratio) while General Motors and Chrysler have an inefficient dealer network (i.e., a lower ratio).
- On a personal level, as gasoline approached and then exceeded $4.00 per gallon who among us wasn't paying more attention to our vehicle's miles per gallon (the ratio of total miles driven divided by gallons of fuel consumed)?
- Finally, the obvious ratio for college students is grade point average.

Our point is that ratios are developed in a variety of contexts to help evaluate efficiency and effectiveness. The ratios presented in this chapter should be viewed in the context of being a subset of a larger body of such measures.

The other point we should make about ratios is that the resulting number often has little meaning in an absolute sense. If we determine that, say, the Gross Profit Margin for a company is 35% what does that mean? By itself, it may mean very little. The usefulness of many ratios is when we compare them to things like:

- Past performance.
- Internal goals or expectations.
- Performance of key competitors.
- Industry averages.

EVALUATING STRATEGY USING RATIOS: PART II

In the previous chapter we discussed how the Gross Profit Margin and the Net Profit Margin of Wal-Mart and Neiman Marcus reflect differences in their underlying business strategies. We're going to continue that discussion a bit further here so that we can make an additional point about business strategy and ratio analysis.

Let's introduce a new ratio to measure how effective a company is at generating Sales compared to its Total Assets. That is, what level of Sales do we produce given the size of a company as measured by its investment in Total Assets? This ratio is called the Asset Turnover ratio.

Asset Turnover Ratio = Sales / Total Assets

Now, with a bit of algebra we're going to combine the Net Profit Margin and the Asset Turnover Ratio into a new measure of profitability called Return on Assets, or ROA for short. This is illustrated in Figure 23.1.

Net Income	*	*Sales*	=	*Net Income*
Sales		Total Assets		Total Assets
Net Profit		Asset		Return on Assets
Margin		Turnover		(ROA)

Figure 23.1. Decomposition of Return on Assets (ROA).

Note that if we multiply the Net Profit Margin by the Asset Turnover Ratio the Sales cancels out in the multiplication and we obtain Net Income over Total Assets, or ROA. This has been found to be a useful way to think about how a company earns a return on the money it has invested in the business (i.e., its Total Assets).

We will not repeat our discussion of Wal-Mart and Neiman Marcus from the last chapter, but just recall that Wal-Mart competes on everyday low prices while Neiman Marcus competes based upon providing a unique, upscale shopping experience. In business jargon, Wal-Mart follows a Cost Leadership (meaning low prices) strategy while Neiman Marcus follows a Differentiation (meaning uniqueness) strategy. Table 23.1 (next page) shows how this is reflected in their Gross Profit Margin, Net Profit Margin, Asset Turnover and ROA.

Table 23.1. Comparison of Wal-Mart and Neiman Marcus

		Wal-Mart	*Neiman Marcus*
Gross Profit Margin	Gross Profit / Sales	23.68%	34.53%
(Net) Profit Margin	Net Income / Sales	3.57%	5.78%
Asset Turnover	Sales / Total Assets	2.40	1.39
Return on Assets (ROA)	Net Income / Total Assets	8.54%	8.05%

In the previous chapter we noted that Neiman Marcus would be expected to have a higher Gross Profit Margin because their customers are less price sensitive and expect services and amenities which must be paid for out of Neiman Marcus' Gross Profit. We also noted that Neiman Marcus had a higher Net Profit Margin than Wal-Mart.

With the introduction of several new ratios we can now add some to our story. Note that Wal-Mart has a higher Asset Turnover, 2.40, compared to Neiman Marcus at 1.39. This means that Wal-Mart generates Sales of $2.40 for every $1.00 of Total Assets, while Neiman Marcus only generates Sales of $1.39 for every $1.00 of Total Assets. In business jargon this is sometimes referred to as "volume."

If we look at the last ratio in the table above, ROA, we see that the two achieved quite similar results, Wal-Mart's ROA is 8.54% and Neiman Marcus' is 8.05%, despite taking different paths. Wal-Mart's Net Profit Margin is quite a bit lower but when multiplied by their higher Asset Turnover they achieve a superior ROA. Wal-Mart appeals to the mass market by offering everyday low prices and what they miss in profit margin they make up for with a high volume of sales.

On the other hand, Neiman Marcus has a higher Net Profit Margin, but a smaller volume of business. This should not be interpreted as a mistake, but rather a reflection of their chosen business strategy. When they opted to compete based upon Differentiation, they no doubt knew that only a subset of people would pay higher prices for the luxury of shopping at a very upscale retailer like Neiman Marcus. Their path to a very respectable 8.05% ROA is higher profit margin and lower volume.

My wish to all of you who might like to start a business someday is that you can achieve the holy grail of business strategy which is high profit margins *and* high volume, but what we usually observe is a trade-off between the two. The Wal-Mart's of the world pursuing a Cost Leadership strategy have low profit margins but make up for it with high volume, while the Neiman Marcus' of the world following Differentiation have high profit margins but lower sales volumes. It is not a matter of what is right or wrong but how you choose to play the game (meaning the strategy you choose) and, given your choice, how well you can execute your game plan that matters most.

SOME OTHER USEFUL RATIOS

We're going to switch to my young daughter's favorite store, Claire's, to conclude our discussion of ratios. I'll use the income statement and balance sheet that I've adapted from Claire's to illustrate a total of 10 financial statement ratios classified into four categories. These financial statements appear as Figures 23.2 and 23.3 in this chapter.

It's interesting to note that when my daughter first drug me into a Claire's store several years ago instead of being bored I should have noticed how many other young girls were also infatuated with Claire's. Looking back, I see that the company's stock price was about $9.00 at that time. Approximately three years later the stock was selling for $33.00 per share. I can only wish I had bought Claire's stock the first day Sarah took me to their store. The moral of the story is, even if you are not a professional stock investor sometimes all you have to do is pay attention to the products or services that you or your friends find appealing to find a good investment!

Income Statement
Adapted from Claire's Stores Inc.
Fiscal Year Ended January 28, 2006
Data in 000s

		Legend
Net Sales	$1,369,752	1
Cost of Goods Sold	625,866	2
Gross Profit	743,886	3
Selling, General & Administrative (SG&A) Expenses	484,215	
Operating Income	259,671	
Income Tax Expense	87,328	
Net Income	$172,343	4
Average Number of Common Shares Outstanding	99,048	5

Figure 23.2. Claire's Income Statement.

Balance Sheet
Adapted from Claire's Stores Inc.
Fiscal Year Ended January 28, 2006
Data in 000s

				Legend
ASSETS				
Current Assets:				
Cash		$431,122		
Inventories		113,405		6
Prepaid Expenses		53,480		
Total Current Assets			$598,007	7
Property, Plant & Equipment (PP&E):				
Land and Buildings		18,151		
Furniture, Fixtures, and Equipment		252,346		
Leasehold Improvements		238,817		
Subtotal		509,314		
Less Accumulated Depreciation		(286,595)		
Total PP&E			222,719	
Intangible Assets, Net			56,175	
Other Assets			15,162	
Goodwill			198,638	
Total Assets			$1,090,701	8
LIABILITIES				
Current Liabilities:				
Accounts Payable	$50,242			
Income Taxes Payable	36,708			
Other Accrued Liabilities	92,495			
Total Current Liabilities		$179,445		9
Long-term Liabilities		42,938		
Total Liabilities			$222,383	10
Stockholders' Equity:				
Common Stock		4,974		
Additional Paid-in Capital		63,321		
Retained Earnings		800,023		
Total Stockholders' Equity			868,318	
Total Liabilities and Stockholders' Equity			$1,090,701	8

Figure 23.3. Claire's Balance Sheet.

Table 23.2 lists the category, name of the ratio, definition of the ratio, calculation of the ratio using the legend from the Claire's income statement or balance sheet, and the result for Claire's Company for their fiscal year ended January 28, 2006.

Table 23.2. Calculation of Selected Financial Statement Ratios for Claire's

Category	*Ratio*	*Definition*	*Legend*	*Claire's*
Profitability	Gross Profit Margin	Gross Profit / Net Sales	3 / 1	54.31%
	Net Profit Margin	Net Income / Net Sales	4 / 1	12.58%
	Return on Assets (ROA)	Net Income / Total Assets	4 / 8	15.80%
	Earnings per Share (EPS)	Net Income / Avg. Shares	4 / 5	$1.74
Activity	Asset Turnover	Net Sales / Total Assets	1 / 8	1.26x
	Inventory Turnover	COGS / Inventory	2 / 6	5.52x
	Accounts Receivable Turnover	Net Sales / AR	n/a	n/a
Liquidity	Current Ratio	Current Assets / Current Liabilities	7 / 9	3.33x
Solvency	Debt-to-Total Assets	Total Liabilities / Total Assets	10 / 8	20.39%
Market	Price – Earnings (PE) Ratio	Price per Share / EPS	n/a	17.87x

PROFITABILITY RATIOS

Claire's has an impressive set of profitability ratios. Since we have already introduced the Gross Profit Margin, Net Profit Margin, and Return on Assets (ROA) ratio, we will not repeat that discussion other than to note the Claire's Gross Profit Margin, Net Profit Margin, and ROA exceeds those shown earlier for both Wal-Mart and Neiman Marcus. Who would think that a retailer selling relatively small, inexpensive items and catering to "tweens" could boast such impressive numbers?

Earnings per Share (EPS) is a new ratio so we should elaborate a bit on it. Assume you invested in a lottery pool and won a $10 million lottery pool. How happy are you? Well, if the lottery pool consists only of you and a good friend and you each invested equal amounts, then you own half the winnings and we suspect you are very happy. On the other hand, what if there were lots of people in the lottery pool, like one million people each with equal shares of the winnings. Now your one-millionth share of the winnings comes to a 10 dollar bill; better than nothing but hardly a reason to make plans for early retirement either.

The concept behind Earnings per Share is similar to the lottery pool above. EPS expresses the winnings of a company, that is their Net Income, on a per share of common stock basis so that an owner can see at a glance what portion of the total Net Income is theirs. EPS is probably the most quoted financial statistic of any we have discussed in Financial Accounting. It seems to be the most widely followed measure of a company's profitability and success.

ACTIVITY RATIOS

The second category of ratios introduced in the table above is called activity ratios. Activity ratios relate one item from the income statement, which is activity for a period of time like 1 year, to one item from the balance sheet, which is a balance at a point in time. We should note that the results from calculating activity ratios are usually expressed in terms of the number of "times" the item "turned over," abbreviated with a small "x" next to the ratio's answer.

The Asset Turnover ratio has been introduced earlier so we'll proceed to the two that are new. The *Inventory Turnover* ratio is a measure of how well a firm is utilizing its inventory to generate sales. The higher the inventory turnover ratio the better the firm is doing at managing its inventory level. Claire's is turning their inventory over, that is selling its inventory, 5.52 times during the year. We'll repeat an earlier point about whether this is good or bad by simply saying it depends upon the comparison figure. Without a comparison figure, the best we can see is that generally, within reason, the higher the turnover the better for activity measures.

The third activity measure is the *Accounts Receivable Turnover* ratio, which compares Sales to Accounts Receivables to determine how well a firm is managing its level of Accounts Receivable given the Sales level it is producing. Claire's was a poor choice to illustrate this ratio as they do not report any Accounts Receivable on their balance sheet so we cannot calculate the ratio at all! Things work that way in the real world sometimes and the moral of the story might be that not all ratios apply to all firms all the time. It also seems like good news that Claire's is able to generate impressive profitability figures without having to incur the risk of collecting Accounts Receivable.

LIQUIDITY RATIOS

In an earlier chapter we defined liquidity as "nearness to cash." The meaning might be slightly different here as we are going to say liquidity refers to the company's ability to pay its short-term obligations as they come due. We have limited our liquidity measures to a single ratio, the *Current Ratio,* defined as Current Assets over Current Liabilities. For Claire's, their Current Ratio is 3.33 times, meaning they have $3.33 in Current Assets for every $1.00 in Current Liabilities. Again, a comparison figure would be helpful but a common rule of thumb is that a Current Ratio of 2.0 or greater is a positive sign for the company.

SOLVENCY RATIOS

Solvency is similar to liquidity in that it is trying to gauge a company's ability to pays it debts. Solvency is different from liquidity in that its focus is broader by taking into account all of firm's Liabilities, current and long-term, and comparing them to the firm's Total Assets. The basic idea is that, all other things being equal, the more debt a company has in comparison to its assets, the greater is the risk that the company may be unable to repay its debts as they come due. Claire's *Debt-to-Total Assets* ratio is a modest 20.39%, meaning that about 20% of its Total Assets are financed with debt and the complement, or about 80%, is financed with Equity.

MARKET RATIOS

Market ratios are useful to determine whether the company's stock might be a "good buy." We have chosen to introduce just one market ratio, the *Price-Earnings (PE)* ratio, for the sake of brevity and because the PE ratio is arguably the most common market ratio. Claire's stock market price nearest the date of these financial statements was $31.09 on January 30, 2006. We have already learned that Claire's EPS is $1.74 per share. The PE ratio tells us, based upon the current stock market price, how much investors are willing to pay for each one dollar of earnings. If we divided $31.09 by $1.74 we get 17.87 times, meaning investors are willing to pay $17.87 for each $1 of Claire's current earnings, or 17.87 times its current earnings.

Does this make Claire's a good buy? Well, what might we compare this to? What if Claire's competitors are selling for a PE ratio of, say, 20 times earnings? This would mean Claire's is cheaper than its competitors and could imply that Claire's is a good buy at $31.09. It could also mean that there is a very good reason why Claire's is selling for less than its competitors. Unfortunately, the PE ratio does not give unequivocal answers to such difficult questions! It does yield some insight into such weighty questions, but can only contribute to helping make a decision, not make the decision all by itself.

SUMMARY

This concludes our discussion of FSA. We will end by noting that there are additional ratios commonly used to evaluate companies. Interested readers should continue their studies of FSA by taking Business Finance where these ratios are covered in more depth and breadth. Our purpose here was to briefly acquaint you with the topic.

CHAPTER 24

INTERNAL CONTROLS

INTRODUCTION

This chapter is a brief introduction to the topic of internal controls. We will define internal controls as all the things an organization does to help prevent bad things from taking place, detect bad things that are already taking place, or generally help ensure that only desirable things occur within an organization.

Internal controls may sound like a fancy term, but we can guarantee that every person reading this chapter has been the subject of some form of internal controls—you just didn't realize it or call them internal controls! As we were growing up, we had rules we had to follow in our families so that bad things would not happen to us. As full- or part-time employees in organizations we have rules that we have to follow to help ensure that bad things do not happen to the organization's assets. As one of our students once said, "I guess I knew what controls were before I realized I knew what controls were."

INTERNAL CONTROL ACTIVITIES

We will discuss five, common internal control activities. The first three are typically implemented to help *prevent* bad things from taking place, while

Financial Accounting: A Course for All Majors, pp. 199–205

the last two are designed to *detect* bad things that might already be taking place. Since "bad things" is a bit vague, perhaps we should elaborate. In this context, by bad things we mean fraud (e.g., embezzlement), abuse (e.g., padding a time card or expense report), or unintentional errors (i.e., mistakes).

Perhaps by far the most common and useful internal control activity is *Segregation of Duties*. This really means that no one person should have too much authority. In some small businesses it is common for a single office manager to do all the office work. Sometimes this is unavoidable, but it is also a recipe for disaster. When one person handles all the record keeping, they soon start seeing ways to steal from the organization. We've often seen it start innocently enough when the person makes a mistake and no one detects it. "Hum, if no one caught the mistake perhaps I could make another "mistake" next week and not get caught either."

Here's an example involving bad debts. What if the person recording accounts receivable and bad debts is also the same person who collects payments from customers? This person could collect a cash payment from a customer, pocket the cash, and write the customer's account receivable off as a bad debt.

The point of our discussion is not to give you ideas of ways to steal; our point is to warn you that if you own the company you need to think about Segregation of Duties so that you will not be the next victim of fraud, abuse, or carelessness.

The second internal control activity is proper *Authorizations*. In a small grocery store we heard about they had a system in place that required a supervisor to personally approve all voided cash register transactions. This internal control activity was put in place to prevent employees from ringing up customers, receiving cash payments, improperly voiding the sale, and pocketing the cash. Unfortunately, the supervisor decided she didn't have time to authorize every voided sale so she simply gave the cash register clerk, whom she trusted, her authorization code. The result was a fairly substantial fraud due to improperly voided register transactions.

Had the control been implemented properly, this fraud could have been prevented. However, there is an important lesson here. Internal controls must be designed *and implemented* effectively to prevent or detect fraud. In the grocery store case the design was good, but the control was defeated when the supervisor gave her code to the cash register clerk. She did not implement the control properly.

Another example of Authorizations involves a local city government. A city clerk in a small community received cash payments from residents for their monthly water and sewer bills. There was no system of Authorizations in place so she took it upon herself to pocket some of the cash payments and write-off the customers' accounts receivable balances as bad debts. A better system would have required the city's governing body to authorize the write-off of all bad debts. In this way, the clerk acting alone could have not written off the bad debts, thus concealing that she stole the customers' cash receipts.

A third internal control activity is *Physical Safeguards.* Physical safeguards include locked areas to protect assets like cash or inventory, and passwords or security levels to prevent unauthorized access to computer systems. In a prominent financial statement fraud from several decades ago, the auditors of Miniscribe followed common audit practice at the time (1980s) by locking all of their workpapers in trunks at the end of each day. This was an attempt to implement the concept of Physical Safeguards. Unfortunately, the locks must have been ineffective as the company's managers were able to sneak back into the office after hours, gain access to the workpapers, and manipulate the figures to conceal a massive fraud.

To quote Steinbeck from *Of Mice and Men*, "The best laid plans of mice and men often go astray," and so it is with internal controls. We never said internal controls were 100% effective. In fact, the only certain way to avoid bad things is to avoid all activity. Perhaps it would be better if we said that internal controls are designed to minimize the risks of bad things happening. And, they have to be subject to a cost-benefit test. If we had an unlimited amount of money, we could probably design a system that was nearly foolproof; however, such a system would probably not be reasonable for most organizations so we "do the best we can" given the resources available to us.

Another example of Physical Safeguards is the "cage" at a casino. In a casino, chips are currency so the business goes to great lengths to make sure they are kept in a secure area. If any of you work in a manufacturing business you may have observed similar, locked areas where the business keeps valuable materials used in the manufacturing process. Some of you work in healthcare. In that setting it is important that the drugs be kept in secure areas as they obviously have a high value on the street, not to mention the harmful effects of a patient not receiving their proper medications. Finally, there is no better place to observe Physical Safeguards than in a correctional facility (i.e., prison). The reason for such controls is rather obvious in this setting.

Segregation of Duties, proper Authorizations, and Physical Safeguards are largely designed to be preventative in nature. That is, they are implemented to prevent bad things from occurring in the first place. The remaining two activities tend to be more focused on detecting bad things that are occurring.

Independent Checks means another party periodically checks the work of others. In a bank setting employees are usually required to take mandatory vacations at least annually. A primary purpose of this rule is so that another person will have to step into that position and in doing so serves as an Independent Check on the other employee's work. Some fairly substantial frauds have gone on for years because no one ever checked on an employee's work.

Another example of Independent Checks is provided by an organization's internal auditing function. At the *Topeka Capitol Journal* an office clerk was recently convicted of stealing more than $400,000 in cash receipts from customers. Her scheme was quite simple. When customers paid cash, she took the money. After several years a team of internal auditors was reviewing her work and noticed that the ratio of cash-to-checks in her office was much lower (lower because she was taking the cash and not depositing it in the company's accounts, but she was not messing with the customers' checks) than in other newspapers owned by the same company. Although the organization would most certainly have liked to prevent this fraud, Independent Checks did (finally) detect the fraud that was occurring.

The final internal control activity we will discuss is *Documentation*. Documents help establish an audit trail so that transactions can be verified for accuracy. A time card is a form of Documentation that most of us can relate to. The number of hours reported on the time card should be consistent with the number of hours reported on the pay stub. In addition, a good practice is to require a supervisor to approve all time sheets, which is another example of proper Authorizations.

Documentation is not perfect. A local school district recently incurred a loss on a construction contract. The contractor had been required to have a performance bond guaranteeing that if they could not complete the job then the bonding company would step in and see that the work was completed satisfactorily. The performance bond in this case had to be filed at the local county courthouse before the work could begin. All of this was apparently done and the school district even checked with the courthouse to make sure the contractor had filed the performance bond. When the contractor left the job unfinished, the school district called the bonding company who said they had never issue the contractor a bond for this job. When the school district went to the courthouse to get a copy of the bond, it was immediately apparent upon personal inspection that the bond had been forged. The case was turned over to the Kansas Bureau of Investigation and the contractor was charged with forgery, among other things. In this case, the Documentation did not prevent the fraud from occurring but it did serve as a key piece of evidence to prosecute the fraudster.

CONTROL OBJECTIVES OF THE FINANCIAL ACCOUNTING SYSTEM

Since all financial transactions should be recorded in the financial accounting system, a properly functioning accounting system can also help prevent and detect bad things like fraud and abuse from occurring. A properly functioning accounting system should accomplish the following six control objectives.

First, all transactions recorded in the accounting system should be *Valid* transactions. Throughout this course we have discussed transactions and merely assumed that they were, in fact, legitimate transactions. A rather simple way to fraudulently inflate revenue is to simply record an entry for a purely fictitious credit sale—increase Assets (Accounts Receivable) and increase Equity (Revenue). Obviously, we will never collect the Account Receivable because there really isn't any customer, but that is a story for another day. Our point here is that a Valid transaction means that entries recorded in the books should correspond with events that actually took place.

Second, the accounting system should include a *Complete* list of all transactions. Companies have sometimes conveniently forgotten to record, for example, Accounts Payable or other Liabilities. The fraud at Enron was extremely sophisticated but at one level very simple—Enron had borrowed a lot of money and found a way to avoid reporting the debt on its balance sheet. Its accounting system did not reflect a Complete list of all the money that Enron owed to creditors.

In a sense, Completeness is the opposite of Validity. Validity means everything recorded actually took place in the manner we have described; completeness means that everything that took place was in fact recorded. I'm reminded of a church phrase here, "Forgive me for everything I have done (e.g., recording invalid transactions or sins of commission) and everything I have failed to do (e.g., failing to record transactions or sins of omission)."

Validity and Completeness are overriding concerns in the accounting system, but our list is not quite complete. All transactions should also be properly *Valued*. That is, the proper amount should be recorded for all transactions. Miniscribe violated this control objective when they recorded bricks as inventory and valued them as if they were computer hard disk drives. With respect to Valuation, we are usually most concerned that a company has Overstated Assets or Understated Liabilities, since these are two ways to artificially inflate the company's financial position.

Fourth, all transactions should be properly *Classified*. This one may be a bit more difficult to comprehend. What if we won the lottery but reported on my personal income statement that the lottery winnings were "Wages and Salary Income." The reader would get the impression that we have a much, much better job than we really do. The point is that if a Revenue source is a one-time, or nonrecurring, event then we should communicate that to the reader so that they will not expect the same thing to occur again next year. Companies sometimes have a bad habit of reporting one-time, good news events as though they are going to be repeated!

The reverse is usually true with Expenses. Assume a company has Expenses that exceed Revenues so they have a negative profit. They might report some of their Expenses as "Loss Due to Flooding" even though they did not experience a flood loss merely to try to convince readers that their large expenses are a one-time problem and will not be repeated.

Notice that the pattern here is to mislead readers into thinking good things (i.e., lottery winnings) are just part of normal operations and will be repeated, while bad things (i.e., bloated and inefficient operations) are one-time events that will not be repeated.

Fifth, all transactions in an accounting system should be properly *Authorized*. Proper authorization helps ensure that all transactions recorded in the accounting system are Valid.

Sixth, *Timing* is a crucial issue when using the Accrual Basis of Accounting. As you know by now, Revenue should not be recognized until we have met the Revenue Recognition Principle Conditions and all Expenses should be reported according to The Matching Principle. Timing is the essence of The Accrual Basis of Accounting as it attempts to report all of an organization's accomplishments (i.e., Revenue) and efforts (i.e., Expenses) in the proper time period so that the resulting measure of profit (Revenue – Expenses = Net Income) will be a meaningful measure of how well the company did for a particular period.

The typical abuse we observe in Financial Accounting is that firms want to accelerate the recognition of Revenues (i.e., report Revenues too early) and defer the recognition of Expenses (i.e., report Expenses too late).

SUMMARY

This chapter was intended to give the reader a brief overview of the important topic of internal controls. We talk about companies and organizations but what if it was your money? Wouldn't you want a strong system of internal controls to help ensure that your resources weren't stolen or misused? This is really the essence of internal controls.

Because of the nature of the industry, a casino is probably the best place one can visit to see this chapter come to life. The next time you visit a casino (if you're so inclined) just look around and you will observe multiple forms of internal controls. A casino has a high level of risk due to the amount of cash and cash equivalents (i.e., chips) involved in their business, the high volume of transactions, and the mindset of customers which is to "beat the house." As a result, the gaming industry spends a great deal more on internal controls than, say, a hotel simply because their risk of loss due to fraud, abuse, and employee error is much higher.

This concludes our course in Financial Accounting. Our overall goal for this course is to improve your financial literacy so that you can benefit from financial stability. Accounting is often called the language of business or, as we prefer, the universal language of world commerce. A secondary goal is that our course has helped you learn this language so that you can be a more productive producer and consumer.

Regardless of your major, we wish you success in your career. This has been Financial Accounting: A Course for All Majors.

APPENDIX I

Debits and Credits

INTRODUCTION

Over the past 15 years it seems as though we've witnessed a sometimes quiet, sometimes noisy debate over how best to teach the first course in Financial Accounting. One of the most fundamental, and controversial, elements of this debate has been whether to use debits and credits in the first course in Financial Accounting.

We have used the traditional, debit and credit approach, we have been advocates of this approach, and we may someday again advocate this approach. For now, however, we believe a better approach for a first course in accounting for all majors is to avoid debits and credits.

If we've learned anything by watching this debate it is that few on either side are likely to be persuaded by any argument we could offer here. Our book is designed for those who are willing to teach this course without debits and credits. The justification for this approach is that we feel the language of debits and credits is often a major impediment to learning, especially when these terms are introduced at an early stage in the course.

Appendix I is primarily for those students who will be taking another course in accounting. Obviously, this would be all business majors. It would also include those who are pursuing a minor in business or accounting. Finally, some majors may require an additional course or courses in accounting as part of their degree requirements. We offer this chapter for those students so that they will not feel as though they are "behind" when their next accounting instructor dives into debits and credits and journal entries on the first day of class.

DEBITS AND CREDITS

In Financial Accounting debit means left and credit means right. No more, no less. If you are especially curious about the "how and why" we refer you to the article referenced at the end of this Appendix.

ACCOUNT RULES

In Financial Accounting we use the term account rules to mean how we record increases and decreases in accounts using the terminology of debits and credits. Essentially, debits and credits are a rather elegant way to communicate how an accounting event affects the accounting equation. Debits and credits take the place of, and are a substitute for, the plus and minus terminology used in this textbook. This alternative way to record transactions does not change any of the concepts we have covered in Chapters 1–24. Debits and credits are simply an alternative way to communicate the same information.

Table AI.1 summarizes the account rules for the most common types of accounts. Is there an easy way to remember these? We've heard some useful ways over the years, but here's our approach. Think about the accounting equation:

$$\text{Assets} = \text{Liabilities} + \text{Equity}$$

Assets are on the left-hand side of the equal sign, debit means left, so a debit increases Assets. The opposite would decrease Assets, meaning a credit decreases Assets.

Liabilities and Equity are on the right-hand side of the equal sign, credit means right, so a credit will increase Liability accounts and permanent Equity accounts like Contributed Capital and Retained Earnings. The opposite, meaning a debit, would decrease these accounts.

The temporary equity accounts, Revenues, Expenses, and Dividends, could be confusing but do not need to be. Revenues increase Equity so they follow the same account rules as Equity accounts above. Expenses and Dividends both decrease Equity so their account rules are the opposite of Equity—to increase Expenses or Dividends we would debit them (which effectively decreases Equity just as we have learned throughout this course).

Table AI.1. Account Rules for Debit and Credits

Account	*Increase / +*	*Decrease / -*	*Normal Balance*
Assets	Debit	Credit	Debit
Contra-Asset	Credit	Debit	Credit
Liabilities	Credit	Debit	Credit
Contributed Capital	Credit	Debit	Credit
Retained Earnings	Credit	Debit	Credit
Contra-Equity	Debit	Credit	Debit
Revenues	Credit	Debit	Credit
Contra-Revenue	Debit	Credit	Debit
Expenses	Debit	Credit	Debit
Dividends	Debit	Credit	Debit

Contra accounts always reduce the account they are related to so their account rules are always the opposite of their related account.

The right-hand column above labeled Normal Balance is a bit redundant. The Normal Balance of an account is merely that which increases the account.

THE FORMAT OF JOURNAL ENTRIES

In a traditional Financial Accounting class when we record the effect of an accounting event on the accounting equation it is written in what is called journal entry format as follows:

Account to be Debited	$xxx	
Account to be Credited		$xxx

Let's look at a few examples. Let's say we want to record a credit sale for $100:

Accounts Receivable	$100	
Sales		$100

Or, an accrual for wages of $100 incurred but not yet paid:

Wages Expense	$100	
Wages Payable		$100

The entry to record bad debt expense of $100 from chapters 13 and 14 involves a contra-asset account:

Bad Debt Expense	$100	
Allowance for Bad Debts		$100

We could go on, but there's little to be gained from the exercise. The standard journal entry format is simply to left justify the account or accounts to be debited and write them first. Beneath them we indent a bit and write the account or accounts to be credited.

A FINAL NOTE—T ACCOUNTS

Another tool that is frequently used in accounting classes is called a t-account. We draw a large T, put the account title above the T and then use the left-hand side to record debits to that account and the right-hand side to record credits. This is shown in Figure AI.1:

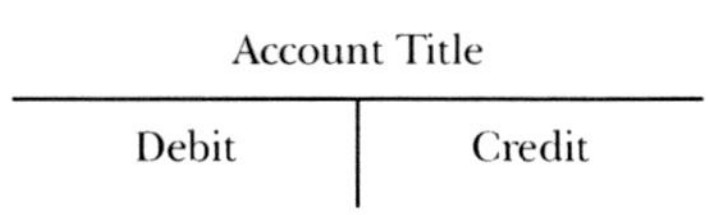

Figure AI.1: T-Account

Nothing new here—debit means left, credit means right. No need to make this difficult.

SUMMARY

If you are going to take more accounting courses, there is no denying that you will encounter debits and credits. They are an extremely useful communication device in the accounting profession. This brief overview should suffice, however, to help you transition to this new way of doing things. Remember, the concepts are the same only the labels have been changed (i.e., pluses and minuses have been replaced with debits and credits). We wish you well in your future accounting courses.

For the curious few in the audience who would like to know the "why" associated with debits and credits and not just the "how," we refer you to O'Bryan, Casey, and Woodburn (2003).

REFERENCE

O'Bryan, D., B. Casey, C. Woodburn. (2003, Fall). The algebra underlying accounting rules: A teaching note. *Accounting Instructors' Report*. Retrieved from http://college.hmco.com/accounting/resources/instructors/air/fall_2003/obryan.htm

APPENDIX II

Transaction Analysis Quick Reference Guide

Appendix II is designed to be a quick reference guide to transaction analysis for operating, investing, and financing activities. We begin with some basic rules of transaction analysis.

- *The accounting equation must always remain in balance.* This is the most fundamental rule as it provides the mathematical structure for transaction analysis.
- Since the accounting equation must always remain in balance, if you change one item in the accounting equation then you must change at least one other item. That is, *every transaction will affect at least two accounts in the accounting equation.*

Now, there are some combinations that will, in a mathematical sense, ensure the accounting equation remains in balance:

- If you increase an Asset, then you may (a) decrease another Asset, (b) increase Liabilities, or (c) increase Equity.
- If you decrease an Asset, then you may (a) increase another Asset, (b) decrease Liabilities, or (c) decrease Equity.
- If you increase a Liability, then you may (a) decrease another Liability, (b) decrease Equity, or (c) increase Assets.
- If you decrease a Liability, then you may (a) increase another Liability, (b) increase Equity, or (c) decrease Assets.

- If you increase Equity, then you may (a) decrease another Equity, (b) decrease Liabilities, or (c) increase Assets.
- If you decrease Equity, then you may (a) increase another Equity, (b) increase Liabilities, or (c) decrease Assets.

Those rules seem complicated and wordy. Let's see if we can't refine them a bit. It looks like that in every single case above, if we change one element then we can always do the opposite to the same element and the accounting equation will remain in balance.

> Rule 1: You may increase one account within an element (Asset, Liabilities, or Equity) and decrease another account within the same element.

> Rule 2: If you change an Asset, then you may make the same directional change to a Liability or Equity.

Note that these Rules tell you what you may do but they also implicitly tell us what we can*not* do. For example, a violation of Rule 1 would be to increase Cash and increase Land since that is increasing two accounts within the same element (Assets). A violation of Rule 2 would be to increase Inventory and decrease Accounts Payable because the directional change to the Asset, Inventory, is not the same as the directional change to the Liability, Accounts Payable.

> Rule 3: If you change a Liability, then you may make the same directional change to an Asset, or the opposite to an Equity account.

A violation of Rule 3 would be to increase a Liability and increase Equity. Another violation would be to increase a Liability and decrease an Asset.

> Rule 4: If you change an Equity account, then you may make the same directional change to an Asset, or the opposite to a Liability account.

If you follow Rules 1-4 then the accounting equation will remain in balance. This is a necessary but not sufficient condition for a correct answer. If the way you record a transaction results in the accounting equation being out of balance, then your answer must be wrong. On the other hand, maintaining balance in the accounting equation does not guarantee you have recorded the transaction correctly. For example, what if you recorded the collection of an Account Receivable by increasing Cash and decreasing Land? The accounting equation will balance because you increased one Asset and decreased another Asset (permissible under Rule 1), but this hides the fact that you decreased the wrong Asset (Land instead of Accounts Receivable).

We should also note that Rules 1–4 state what you *may* do. They are a list of permissible ways transactions can be recorded.

OPERATING ACTIVITIES

Table AII.1 lists some common transactions associated with the operating activities of a firm followed by the correct way to record the transaction. Remember that operating activities are those related to the day-to-day activities of making sales to customers and paying for the related costs of doing business.

Table AII.1: Transaction Quick Reference Guide for Operating Activities

Transaction	*Assets =*	*Liabilities +*	*Equity*
Provided services and rec'd cash payment.	+ Op. Cash		+ Revenue
Billed customer for services provided on credit.	+ Accounts Receivable (AR)		+ Revenue
Collected account receivable from above.	+ Op. Cash; – AR		
Rec'd cash for services to be provided later.	+ Op. Cash	+ Unearned Revenue	
Provided service for the transaction above.		- Unearned Revenue	+ Revenue
Cash payment for expenses.	– Op. Cash		– Expenses
Rec'd bill for operating cost; will be paid later.		+ Accounts Payable	– Expense
Paid the bill above.	– Op. Cash	- Accounts Payable	
Paid a bill in advance / before using the item.	+ Prepaid Item; – Op. Cash		
Consumed the item paid for above.	– Prepaid Item		– Expense
Purchase of Inventory for Cash	– Op. Cash; + Inventory		
Sale of Inventory for Cash—Revenue Part	+ Op. Cash		+ Revenue
Sale of Inventory for Cash—Expense Part	– Inventory		– Cost of Goods Sold

INVESTING ACTIVITIES

Investing activities involve buying and later disposing of long-term assets (those with an expected useful life of more than 1 year). We will also cover the process of cost allocation related to these long-term assets. Table AII.2 summarizes the key transactions related to investing activities.

Table AII.2: Transaction Quick Reference Guide for Investing Activities

Transaction	*Assets =*	*Liabilities +*	*Equity*
Paid cash for long-term asset, Equipment.	+ Equipment; – Inv. Cash		
Allocated part of Equipment cost to expense.	– Equipment (Contra-Acct.)		– Expense
Sold Equipment for Gain (1)	+ Inv. Cash; – Equipment		+ Gain
Sold Equipment for Loss (2)	+ Inv. Cash; – Equipment		– Loss

(1) Cash received > Book value of equipment; difference equals Gain.

(2) Cash received < Book value of equipment; difference equals Loss.

When you buy a long-term asset you record its cost, including all the costs incurred to get the asset ready for its intended use (e.g., transportation, installation).

During the time the asset is being used to help generate revenue, the asset is subject to cost allocation procedures. This simply means we allocate a portion of the cost of the asset as a charge to expense each period. Land is not subject to cost allocation because it has an unlimited life. Cost allocation is called Depreciation for most tangible assets, Amortization for intangible assets, and Depletion for natural resources. A contra-asset, Accumulated Depreciation, is used to record Depreciation and a similar account may be used for Amortization or Depletion.

When the asset is later sold, we will probably receive an amount that differs from the asset's recorded book value (cost minus accumulated cost allocation). If we receive more than the asset's book value we call the excess a gain, and if we receive less the deficit is called a loss.

FINANCING ACTIVITIES

There are two primary ways to finance a business, debt or equity. Financing activities include borrowing and repaying the debt plus interest. It also includes issuing stock, paying dividends and potentially repurchasing stock. Table AII.3 provides the quick reference guide for financing activities.

Table AII.3: Transaction Quick Reference Guide for Financing Activities

Transaction	*Assets* =	*Liabilities* +	*Equity*
Borrowed money.	+ Fin. Cash	+ Notes Payable	
Repaid amount borrowed.	– Fin. Cash	– Notes Payable	
Paid interest on borrowed funds.	– Op. Cash		– Interest Exp.
Issued Stock	+ Fin. Cash		+ Contributed Capital
Repurchase Stock	– Fin. Cash		– Treasury Stock
Pay Dividend	– Fin. Cash		– Dividends

We should note that the payment of interest on borrowed money is classified as an Operating Cash Outflow. However, since interest is related to debt, and debt is a financing activity we will cover it here.

ABOUT THE AUTHOR

David O'Bryan is a professor in the Department of Accounting, Kelce College of Business, at Pittsburg State University (Kansas). He has received two university-wide teaching awards and in 2002 was recognized as the Kansas Society of CPAs Accounting Educator of the Year.

David teaches a variety of courses at Pittsburg State University (PSU) including Financial Accounting, Intermediate Financial Accounting, Advanced Financial Accounting, Fraud Examination, Financial Statement Analysis (MBA level), and Management Control Systems (MBA level). The Financial Accounting course at PSU is an elective for general education majors and more than 50% of the students in a typical section are non-business majors. Teaching Financial Accounting to a general education audience was the inspiration for this textbook.

In addition to his teaching responsibilities, David has published in numerous scholarly publications including the *Journal of Accounting Education*, *Journal of Accounting Case Research*, *Behavioral Research in Accounting*, *Advances in Accounting*, and the *Journal of Business Finance and Accounting*. His coauthored article in Volume 18, Issue 2, of the *Journal of Accounting Education*, titled "Using Accounting Equation Analysis to Teach the Statement of Cash Flows in the First Financial Accounting Course," was recently noted on the list of Top 25 articles in that journal. This article forms the procedural basis for his approach to the first course in Financial Accounting.

David earned his BBA in Business Administration and MBA in General Administration from Pittsburg State University, and earned his PhD in Accountancy from the University of Missouri at Columbia. His professional designations include the CPA, CMA, and CFE.

CPSIA information can be obtained at www.ICGtesting.com
Printed in the USA
LVOW071921230912

299958LV00002B/3/P